WAYWARD SON

Travels and Reflections

DAVID DRAYER

ROUTE 33 PRESS

Wayward Son: Travels and Reflections

Copyright © 2018 by David Drayer

Published in the United States of America by Route 33 Press.
ISBN: 978-0-9892827-6-5
Library of Congress Control Number: 2018901518

Cover & interior design: Brian E.W. McNulty
Author photo: Jonathan Shimmons
Photo credits:
"A Good Bar"– Samuel J. Garza
"Natural Inspiration," "Love Bites," and "A Long Walk" – Jeanne Drayer
"What Now?" – Thierry Klann
"To What End?" – Susan Kane
"Football Philosophy" – Courtesy of *The Observer* [La Grande, OR]

All columns originally appeared in the *Leader-Vindicator* [New Bethlehem, PA] from 2015 - 2017.

*This book is dedicated to my mom, Norma
(Horner) Drayer, who encouraged me to dream
and convinced me that big dreams could come true.*

CONTENTS

ACKNOWLEDGMENTS

A very special thanks to my sister and brother-in-law, Jeanne and Chuck, for giving me a cozy place to hang my hat while I put this book together.

Once again, thanks to my first readers—Thierry Klann, Janet K. Stadulis, Jeanne Drayer, and Susan Kane— for their invaluable feedback.

INTRODUCTION

"**I**t all starts with a tiny, stupid idea," says entrepreneur, Richie Norton, "then one thing leads to another, and suddenly, you find something *amazing*."

I can attest to this. In fact, it's practically the story of my life.

This collection of travel blogs and newspaper columns is a perfect example. It began on a blisteringly hot day in the summer of 2013. I was living in the Washington, DC Metro Area and trying to get home after an exhausting week of work. Rush hour was brutal, and to make matters worse, I was on my motorcycle, sweating through my business clothes and feeling sick from the exhaust fumes. Even though I was 10 miles from my apartment, I had the stupid idea to get off at the next exit and take the first open road I could find. Of course, it took me in the opposite direction of where I lived, but it felt so good to be moving that I just kept going.

That foolish notion—chronicled in the first chapter of this collection—led to the series of events responsible for the pieces gathered here. After that first impromptu motorcycle trip, I made a habit of taking off every Friday afternoon and spending the entire weekend going wherever the road took me. Roaming the backwoods and exploring the small towns of Virginia, West Virginia, Maryland, and Pennsylvania, I started writing an informal travel blog called *Drayer's Notebook*. These adventures (and misadventures) kick off this anthology and make up the first nine chapters.

The rest of the book is the end result of what was probably the stupidest idea of my entire life. I decided to quit my job and spend a year writing my next novel, riding the wheels off my motorcycle, and doing whatever else I damn well pleased. This stoke of lunacy is recounted in the aptly-titled chapter "Why the Hell Not?" and, eventually, it led me back to my hometown in western Pennsylvania. There, I began writing a column—*Tales of a Wayward Son*—for a small, weekly newspaper. The gig paid next to nothing, but it made my day to hear that my column made a reader laugh out loud while pondering peculiar nicknames and superstitions, or caused another to take a few moments to think about what matters in life and what doesn't. Even better was finding out I had inspired someone to visit a long-lost relative, take a road trip, or go after a dream.

My search for "A Good Bar" starts the columns which go on to explore the comforts and difficulties of returning to small-town life after nearly three decades of living in major cities across the country.

I hope my stupid ideas have resulted in a book that brings a smile to your face and encourages you to do something foolish ... and amazing.

Enjoy!

DRAYER'S NOTEBOOK

Perspective is Everything

To what end?

Tales of a **Wayward Son**
David Drayer

DESTINATION UNKNOWN

Motorcycles are not meant to sit in traffic. It's just wrong.
I am gridlocked on the westbound 66 somewhere between Fairfax and Falls Church in northern Virginia. Burning up in the July heat and on the verge of hurling from breathing in exhaust fumes, I've had enough.

I ignore the annoyed expressions of commuters in air-conditioned cars and ride the berm of the road to the next exit. I wander bleary-eyed through the urban sprawl until I find an open road. I don't know where I'm going, and I don't care. I'm moving, by God, with my necktie flying behind me like a banner advertising freedom. The farther and faster I go, the better I feel.

Taking whatever road looks interesting, I ride until the shopping malls and chain restaurants give way to pastures lined with wooden fences and placards announcing Civil War battlegrounds. Stone houses and old-money estates. Livestock in the fields. Wine vineyards. Fresh air!

I realize I am no longer running from something but towards something, though I can't say exactly what that is. I just don't want to stop.

The next thing I know, I'm crossing the state line into West Virginia. For several miles at a time, I have the road to myself as it snakes through the forest. When the sun starts to go down, the temperature drops. The early evening quickly goes from warm to chilly to cold. The business attire I'm required to wear at work offers no protection. I have gone too far to go back home, so I pull off at the side of the road and check my phone for the nearest motel.

No signal. Yikes!

That's a bit of a wake-up call. I have about a half-hour before the sun goes down. If I don't find a place to spend the night soon, I am going to be in a bit of trouble. I went through a few tiny towns earlier, but none of them appeared to have a motel, and having taken roads willy-nilly, I doubt I'd be able to backtrack anyway.

I keep heading west. According to the occasional sign, I am in the Monongahela National Forest. A black bear lumbers across the road in front of me like another reminder from the universe that my impulsive nature tends to get me into trouble. "Alright already!" I say, aloud, "I hear you. I'm looking for a room right now."

It's dark when I arrive in the town of Elkins. Freezing now, I pull into the first motel I see. It's a standard budget chain that I've stayed in many times, but there is something strange about this one. The lobby is huge and cavernous; the front desk is small and tucked in a corner. There is not a soul in sight. I ring the service bell and wait another couple of minutes, blowing into my hands to warm them.

I ring the bell again and a woman finally comes out from the back looking tired, disheveled, and annoyed. I try making conversation, but filling out the paperwork seems to take her full concentration. "Is there a good place nearby for dinner?" I ask.

"There are lots of places around," she mumbles.

For both of our sakes, I hope her shift is almost over.

The peculiar atmosphere of the place goes beyond the lobby. From the groaning of the large, rickety elevator to the empty hallways and weird layout of the floors, there is something eerie about it. It feels like it's pretending to be something it's not.

The sensation intensifies when I get to my room. The mirror and sink are next to the bed. The bathroom door is metal and it opens to a commercial toilet with handrails and a yellow-tiled shower stall with a flimsy, plastic curtain. Suddenly, I understand the floor plan, the lobby, and the creepy feeling. This place used to be a hospital.

I look back at my room and it is too easy to imagine a hospital bed surrounded by monitors.

I wonder if it's too late to get my money back.

One of the best things about being a writer—I have told many creative writing classes over the years—is that nothing is wasted on you. Even the most unpleasant experiences are fodder for future stories.

For example, say you have to spend the night at a creepy motel and wake up at 4:00 AM in a cold sweat with your heart hammering madly from a nightmare. If you are a writer, you don't have to try to forget it, go back to sleep, and pray for daylight. No, sir! You grab the notepad and pen from the night-stand and describe the details of the dream: the empty eyes and tattered hospital gown of the old woman standing over you or the terror of being chased through the corridors of an old hospital by an unseen entity.

And when you go out to your motorcycle early the next morning to find the temperature has dropped drastically to an unseasonal 45 freaking degrees, you start making mental notes, beginning with the internal dialogue, one part of your mind calling you an idiot for getting yourself into such a predicament, the other boldly arguing that this is all part of the adventure.

After figuring out where the nearest retail store can be found, you saddle up and head in that direction to buy some warmer clothes. During the coldest 27-minute ride of your life, you pay attention to how the wind cuts through your thin dress clothes and see how many different ways you can describe a frozen face, frostbit ears, numb fingers, and how Walmart can look like heaven.

You find humor in the outfit purchased purely for warmth and wind protection. From the clearance rack, a sweatshirt with a Superman logo, fleece-lined jeans, a faux leather jacket with a fur collar, and from the hunting section, a camouflage face mask, duck boots, and fluorescent orange gloves. You note how conspicuous you feel walking through the parking lot in this getup and how bizarre it is that no one even notices.

It is late afternoon. I'm in Warm Springs, Virginia, looking for the pools of water that gave the town its name.

Though I have warmer clothes now and the temperature has risen considerably since this morning, I haven't completely shaken the chill and a dip in mineral waters that come out of the ground at 98 degrees is inviting.

There are a few other cars in the parking lot when I pull into the spa where Thomas Jefferson was once a frequent visitor. The octagon-shaped Gentleman's Pool House was built in 1761 and is said to be the oldest spa structure in the country. The adjacent Ladies' Pool House was built 75 years later. I am surprised to find both looking run-down and in bad need of a paint job.

The place is open for business though. Warm and hot springs were once believed to have medicinal powers, healing everything from serious diseases to easing sore joints and muscles. Today, many people still believe in their magic.

After paying the attendant $17.00 for an hour-long soak, I go into the Gentleman's Pool House. A handful of other guys are scattered throughout the large pool, clinging to neon-colored "floaties" that look out of place in the ramshackle building. Clothing is optional during adult hours, which is good because I certainly didn't think to pick up a bathing suit at Walmart this morning.

I follow the wooden, moss-covered steps into the pool and swim toward a couple of floaties. The water is over six and a half feet deep. It has a sulfur smell to it, but it's warm, soothing, and crystal clear, allowing me to see to the rocky bottom.

I imagine Thomas Jefferson coming here. I wonder what the writer of the Declaration of Independence, creator of countless inventions and agricultural advancements, thought about while soaking in these waters. Or was this a place he came to allow his busy mind to go quiet?

My thoughts drift to the nightmares I had last night. Were they the result of a haunted motel or an overactive imagination?

I honestly don't know.

I do know one thing though. Weekend motorcycle trips like this are going to become a regular part of my life. I like the idea of going wherever the road takes me on a Friday afternoon and following it throughout the weekend. From now on, however, I will be wearing proper riding gear and have a change of clothes and whatever else I might need on the road.

WAYWARD SON: TRAVELS AND

ROADS

With the saddlebags packed for a weekend trip, I go into work extra early and manage to clock out in time to dodge the afternoon traffic. By 4:00, I am well on my way; I even left a fresh set of dress clothes hanging in my cubicle so I can go to the office on Monday morning from wherever I happen to be. I roll the throttle back, savoring the shot of adrenaline as highways turn into byways and I know my escape is complete. It is safe to slow down, to breathe, to soak up the sun, the trees, and the open fields of the Virginia countryside.

I find myself thinking of the book *Blue Highways*, which is basically the journal of a man who travels across America on back roads. He talks about the joy of going somewhere and how no one can judge you by your past because when you're on the road, there is no past, no yesterday. There is only who you are and how you live right now.

It's no wonder the road is so often used as a metaphor for life. Even following a map or a GPS, there is no way of knowing what's over the horizon. The countless roads I've traveled—both literally and figuratively—took me to places, led me to jobs, and introduced me to people I couldn't have possibly predicted or prepared for.

The sun is going down as I ride into the little town of Martinsburg, West Virginia. A banner hovers over Main Street announcing that the Mountain State Apple Harvest Festival kicks off tonight. A band is warming up in the town square. I'm pretty sure I have found my stop for the night. I park my bike and wander around a bit. Families loaded down with folding chairs and picnic baskets follow the music. Teenagers linger as far away from their parents as possible, some alone, most in small groups. They try to remain aloof, but the girls have obviously dressed for the event in full makeup, new jeans, and skirts. Even though the music is not *their* kind of music, the girls follow it too, and the boys, of course, follow the girls.

I take the long way to the square, noting the usual small-town storefronts—hardware, pharmacy, restaurants—and a couple not so typical, a store of fine chocolates and a pawn shop advertising guns, gold and silver.

The band is good. They are five guys playing a mix of pop, rock, R&B, timeless songs that everyone knows. The crowd is still in the awkward stage of standing around with their hands in their pockets, smiling, nodding. Standing in front of me, a woman with a long gray ponytail grabs the arm of a thirteen or fourteen-year-old girl and says, "Let's get this thing going!"

"Gram, no!" the teenager says, holding her ground, embarrassed.

"Come on, you didn't spend an hour doing your hair just to stand here."

The girl doesn't budge. Grandma is momentarily dejected, but when the band starts doing KC and the Sunshine Band, she starts dancing through the crowd and onto the lawn, loud and proud. She's not alone for long. A group of little kids join her. Then a couple other women join in, one with a baby on her hip. They are getting into it, singing, "Shake your booty, shake your boot-ay!"

A guy in his mid-fifties, dressed in a tee-shirt, jeans, and blindingly white tennis shoes introduces himself to me as Jim something or other. "I'm hoping to represent West Virginia in the House," he says, "so I'm out here saying hi to folks." I tell him I am not a resident of West Virginia and am just passing through.

"Well then, welcome to our great state," he says and informs me that I have picked the right time to pass through. "There's all kinds of fun stuff going on this weekend. I took a picture of the schedule on my phone," he says, pulling it from his pocket and handing it to me.

I take a cursory look as he tells me he's not from this part of the state and hits a different festival every weekend. "This town's a little smaller than it looked on the Internet," he says with a trace of disappointment. "I pretty near met everyone already." He scans the crowd, nods, and with a sigh, he says, "Yep. Talked to all of them."

Giving him back his phone, I ask if he's ever held office before. He admits that he's new to being a politician and is only running because God called him to do it. "Yeah, my wife and I prayed about all the craziness going on in the country, and so, here I am. Stepping out in faith and obedience."

I don't quite know what to say to that so I just say, "Sounds interesting."

"Let me tell ya, brother, it sure is." Just then, a young couple wanders into the gathering and Jim follows them. "I'm running for the House of Representatives," he tells them, "and I'm just out here saying hi to folks."

A very drunk guy bumps into me and apologizes.

"No problem," I say. He continues standing there, looking at me. "No worries," I say, "You're fine."

"Are you mad at me?"

"Nope. Not a bit."

Grandma's little circle of dancers has grown and covers the entire lawn now. He watches them for a moment and glances around the square. He pulls at his whiskered chin. "Everybody's mad at me."

"Probably not everybody," I tell him.

This doesn't seem to register. He turns to me again. "I'm just trying to have fun."

"I can see that."

"Are you mad at me?"

"No, sir."

"I'm just trying to have fun," he says again.

He scuffles off looking disturbingly like "a walker" from the television show, *The Walking Dead*. A policewoman watches him with her hands on her hips. I have a feeling the night is not going to end well for him.

The band wants to know if everyone is having fun. The crowd answers with a cheer and some hoots and hollers. "Does anyone here know how to do the Cupid Shuffle?" the lead singer asks.

Another cheer goes up, and the song begins.

I walk back to the bike and ride off in search of a room for the night. Again, I wonder about the roads we travel, specifically the ones which led to this little town on this particular night, assigning each of us a role: the wannabe politician on a mission from God, the guys in the band, the dancers on the lawn, the families with their picnic baskets, the drunk, the cop, and the weekend wanderer. Where will the road go from here?

PENNSYLVANIA TOWNS WITH PERVY NAMES

I'm in Blue Ball, Pennsylvania.

That's right: Blue Ball.

Instead of heading for southern Virginia or West Virginia, I went north for some reason. It was a bad choice, at first. Too many people and too many cars took the fun right out of it. When I wasn't at a dead standstill amid eight lanes of traffic, I was going 80 to stay with the pack, dodging pot-holes, hostile drivers, and strange grooves in the road, any one of which could have been curtains for a dude on a motorcycle going 80.

But I survived, and here I am in Blue Ball ... which is 40 minutes south of Virginville and just north of Bird in Hand.

Totally not kidding.

But don't worry because Intercourse is only seven miles away and it is right next door to Paradise. Fertility is not far from there either, so be prepared.

Yep. Good old Pennsylvania, my home state, notorious for its pervy names. I grew up in the western part of the state where there are not quite as many, but still, I lived in a little town between Lickingville and Climax.

Here in the south-eastern part of the state, Lancaster County has the lion's share of these names. What adds an extra scoop of bizarre is that this county, about 75 miles west of Philadelphia, is one of the most innocent looking places you can imagine. The endless farms and cornfields are populated by an extraordinary number of Amish families, doing everything in their power to look exactly alike and as un-sexy as possible, clip-clopping every which way in their horse-drawn buggies.

These names color my imagination until all the towns seem to have suggestive names. Baresville sounds like a nudist colony, and Mount Joy, an activity rather than a place.

But enough of that.

As I leave Amish country, I see a kid in a chicken suit jumping up and down on the side of the road, shouting that every passer-by needs to stop and buy some barbequed chicken from the Youth Group that is raising funds for whatever youth groups raise funds for. As I drive slowly by, he points at me and shouts, "You! You need chicken!"

Actually, I have been on the road for several hours, and I am pretty hungry. I think to myself, "That kid's right. I do need chicken." So, I hang a U-turn and buy some chicken, a Styrofoam container of macaroni salad and a Mountain Dew supporting what I am going to assume is a good cause. Finding a nice spot in the shade of a row of pine trees, I pig out.

Cruising along the Susquehanna in Dauphin County, I see the Statue of Liberty in the middle of the river and …

Wait. What?

I try to pull over, but there is no place to stop. Cars and trucks race by on each side of me. I whip off the exit, turn around, and head back. I don't see it this time. Then…there she is: Lady Liberty—or rather a small replica of her on top of what looks like a piece of an old bridge—standing majestically in the middle of the Susquehanna River.

A half-hour later, I come upon the little town of Millersburg which boasts the only surviving ferry service regularly crossing the Susquehanna. According to the surrounding signage, it began in 1825. The commuter boat was powered by men using poles then. Later, a paddlewheel was used, then a steam engine, and in the 1920s, they went to gasoline.

MILLERSBURG, PA

MILLERSBURG, PA

FERRY IS RUNNING

DRIVE DOWN THE HILL

AND ILL COME

AND GET YOU

There is a line of cars and a group of bikers waiting for the vessel's return. "Where does it take you to?" I ask an old fella leaning against his pickup, a wad of tobacco in his cheek.

"Liverpool, Pennsylvania," he tells me.

Looks like I'm going to Liverpool.

The guy tells me it takes 25 minutes for the ferry to arrive when they see people waiting to cross. Stiff from hours on the bike, I use the opportunity to stretch out and walk around. After 40 minutes, there's still no ferry. I walk back over to the old fella, who checks his watch, scratches his bald head, and says, "Something ain't right."

The ferry arrives 10 minutes later and no more than docks before the guy running it (the ferry captain?) walks up to us looking apologetic. Turns out the boat broke down in the middle of the trip. "We got across," he says, "but we can't risk another run until she's repaired. Sorry, folks."

"Will that happen today?" a burly biker wants to know.

"No, sir. Not today. Sorry."

The group is crestfallen. "I really wanted to ride that thing," the biker says to his buddies. "I put it on Facebook and everything."

So...I guess I'm *not* going to Liverpool.

Oh well, maybe some other time. I get back on the road. I want to keep heading north, maybe up through Potter County and on into upstate New York. And why stop there? Why not keep going through the Adirondacks and on into Canada? I have heard Montreal is a great city.

Something in me always wants to keep going, but if I have any intention of being at work on Monday morning, I need to start working my way south, back to the DC area. But the desire is strong. I am on the verge of going rogue. A strain of Springsteen echoes through my mind: "Like a river that don't know where it's flowing/ I took a wrong turn and I just kept going..."

What stops me is the experience from a lifetime of taking risks and living on the edge. The first few days would be exhilarating, I know, but the following weeks almost certainly will not live up to the fantasy unfolding in my mind at the moment.

I have been playing around with a character for my next novel and realize that taking off like this is something he might do. Maybe I should let him go in my place. Let him answer the question, "What happens if you just keep going?"

I like that idea. For now, at least. And hey, if it works out in the fictional world of the novel, maybe I'll give it a shot in real life.

WHY THE HELL NOT

A strong wind roars through the valley under a dark noon sky. I can barely keep the bike on the road and am desperately seeking shelter. A sudden gust of hot air slams me toward the shoulder. Shelter or not, I am going to have to pull off somewhere soon.

I keep going though, pushing it. This storm was not forecasted. If it had been, I would have cancelled the trip or at least stayed closer to civilization. And yet, even fully aware of the danger I am in, some part of me loves the anticipation of the gathering storm, the raw power and wildness of the wind howling through the trees, the electric charge in the air, the pungent smell, flashes of light, and black clouds about to burst.

Luck is on my side today. I spot a country store ahead. Even better, there is a roof over the entrance. A few minutes later, I'm sitting under it drinking a beer out of a paper sack, eating a hot dog, watching the sky flicker as sheets of rain lash the ground. When I was a boy, my mom would pull back the curtains and lift the blinds during a storm. She'd shut off all the lights and gather us on the couch for the show. When we'd jump at a crack of thunder or a bolt of lightning, she'd laugh and even clap sometimes. She said it was better than television and, eventually, we all agreed with her.

It occurs to me that these weekend motorcycle trips are about more than just getting away for a couple of days or unwinding from a busy week. I'm looking for something out here. I don't know what, exactly, but it feels like a couple pieces of the puzzle are missing and I owe it to myself to find them.

Maybe that's what the urge to keep going is all about. It's on me now, but as I've said before, I've been there and done that. The thrill of doing something rash is short-lived, but that doesn't mean I want to resign myself to daydreams of winning the lottery or selling my novels to Hollywood.

Why couldn't I figure out a way to buy myself some real freedom? A whole year, say, to do whatever I felt like doing. It would be so nice to have the time to write the sequel to *Strip Cuts* that I've been dying to get to. Motorcycle trips wouldn't have to end with the weekend and who knows, maybe I could find those missing puzzle pieces if I had all the time in the world to look for them.

So ... what would a year cost?

I'd have to figure all of my living expenses—food, rent, utilities, phone, car, insurance, taxes, everything—for an entire year. At DC prices, it would take forever to save enough, but if I moved back to my hometown in western Pennsylvania, I could live much cheaper and it would be nice to spend a year living close to my family.

I need to come up with that number and add a little cushion to it. Then, it would be a matter of determination. I would have to work all the overtime I could get, tighten my belt, and save every penny I could until I reached that amount.

But it can be done.

So, why not?

Why the hell not?

HELLO KANSAS

I'm cruising across the tall grass prairie of the Flint Hills in Kansas with the wind blowing through my hair. The company I work for needed someone to spend a month in Wichita implementing the training we developed over the winter, and I volunteered. It's been busy, but I'm at the beginning of 4th of July weekend and the next three days are all mine.

It's easy to forget places like this exist during the day to day life back in DC. Nothing but sweet, fertile fields as far as I can see in every direction and all the fresh air I can breathe. It does my heart good. All is well until I get to Lyon County and search in vain for a ghost town I read about. I have the GPS set for a landmark close to where the ruins are supposed to be, so hopefully I will find it from there.

This is my second mistake of the day. The first was forgetting to pick up a map before leaving El Dorado this morning. I always have a map as a backup to the GPS. Plus, it gives me a better visual of where I am ... which would be nice about now. The GPS has me completely turned around after leading me in circles for an hour. It is also killing my phone battery and the AC phone charger in my backpack is no good out here. I haven't seen another living soul during this whole leg of the trip.

The road turns to gravel and then dirt. I shut down the engine and walk around a bit. There are thousands of grasshoppers flitting around. They land on my shirt, in my hair. It's kind of creepy and I think this would make a good beginning to a horror story. I start jotting things down on the notepad that's always in my back pocket, imagining what kind of weirdness could unfold.

Before I creep myself out too much, I get moving again, assuming that this road has to come out somewhere. I have a quarter tank of gas left so there's time...but the clock is ticking. Even before I started looking for the ghost town, I hadn't seen a gas station in a long while.

Once I figure out where I am, I need to start heading west. I have a motel room waiting for me in Dodge City. I reserved it a few days ago after guesstimating where I would be at the end of the first day. After endless calls, I literally reserved the last room in Dodge.

Somehow or another, I do manage to get back to a main road and am whipping west across the plains, looking for a gas station. Thankfully, I find one, fill up, try to buy a map and a DC phone charger. No luck. I take my wall charger into the men's room and plug in over the sink.

According to Google Maps, I am a long, long way from my reserved motel room so I call, and in my friendliest voice, I tell the girl at the front desk my situation and ask if I can cancel my reservation without penalty.

"Ah," she says, "I don't know."

"Well," I say, trying to pretend this isn't an odd response, "do you think you could find out?"

"Ah," she says again, "I'm not sure." Then, without excusing herself, she starts talking to someone in the background. "Some guy wants to cancel his room for the night," she says to whoever she's talking to.

"Is he on hold?" a man's voice asks.

"No."

"Well, put him on hold."

Without warning, I am suddenly listening to the Muzak version of "Raindrops Keep Falling on my Head."

She finally comes back on the line. "If someone comes in wanting your room, we will cancel it."

"Okay, but that doesn't help me much," I say. "I need to know, yes, you will cancel it without charging me or no, you won't."

She repeats what I have said to the guy in the background. He says, "The policy says he can't cancel this late. He has to pay whether he stays or not."

Great. I think about just eating the cost of the room, but I am not likely to find another vacancy on the holiday weekend so I decide to make a run for it. Before I do, I choose the least sad looking piece of pizza circulating under a heat lamp, wolf it down with a Coke, and get back on the road.

It is a long ride. But I have a lot of thoughts in my head to sort through and this is just the way to do it.

SOMEWHERE IN KANSAS

Approaching Dodge City, my mind is full of images from what was once "the wickedest little city" in the wild west, the "cowboy capital," where Wyatt Earp tried to keep order and his friend, the gunslinger, Doc Holliday, gunned down other men with his legendary quick draw. The illusions fade when I drive into a town overrun with fast food restaurants and chain hotels. There's a Walmart. There's a Dollar Store. It looks exactly like any other place.

Dear America,

I hate to bother you on your birthday, but can we make more of an effort to preserve our small towns? Yes, I know we all like convenient, cheap, and quick, but look at the actual cost of that. Our countless little towns are all unique and each has its own history. Why not embrace that? I mean, it is just no fun if every town looks exactly the same.

Sincerely,

Your Wayward, But Loving Son

I can see why my room was the last available. It reeks of stale smoke, there are cigarette holes in the comforter, I can tell they refill their old shampoo and conditioner bottles, and I don't even want to think about where those dark stains on the chair came from. If I were traveling with a woman, I would not subject her to this, but being alone, it meets my bare minimum: the sheets are clean and so is the bathroom. After all, I will only be here long enough to shower and grab a few hours of sleep.

I take an area map (and one for the state of Kansas) from a rack in the motel lobby. The Museum is a mile east, the Boot Hill Casino is three miles northwest and tonight's fireworks display can be best viewed two miles northeast. No big deal except celebration and casino means I'm going to want to drink and, therefore, not drive. Yes, I can walk all those miles but then I'd have to walk them all back and that doesn't sound like much fun after being on the road all day.

The girl I spoke to on the phone earlier is at the front desk. I ask if they have a shuttle service. She stares blankly at me. I repeat the question. She continues to stare like she is trying to figure out what I am. Then she asks, "You mean like a taxi?"

"No." I explain the difference between a taxi and a shuttle.

She makes a face. "Um, no," she says, "we don't have any shuttles. At least, not that I know of, but I think there is a taxi in town."

"That will work," I say. "Could I get a phone number?"

She recites a number from memory, which is impressive until I realize it is the motel phone number.

"No, I mean the number of the taxi service."

"Ahh..." she looks around for help, then says, "I don't have that."

Dear America,

Me again. I won't bother you anymore today, but I have to ask: Why are we not educating our young people? Instead of helping our citizens get a good education, our government straps those who go on to college with high-interest student loans and then makes a profit off of their lifelong struggle to repay the debt.

I don't mean to get all preachy on you, but as a guy who grew up in a poor, working-class town, this really bites. I took my education seriously, went on to become a published author and be gainfully employed. And yet, 20-some years later, I am still paying those student loans with no final payment in sight.

I mean, what the hell?

I don't want to spoil your birthday, but this is important. We have a proud history and I really want to see that continue.

Sincerely,

Your Faithful, but Concerned Son

I look up the taxi service on my phone and get nowhere, which means I either walk or abstain from drinking so I can drive.

In other words, I walk.

Near the museum, a replica of Dodge City as it appeared in the early 1880s is populated with actors dressed as cowboys. A crowd has gathered around the edges to watch as the reenactment of a gunfight is underway. It is well done, complete with fistfights and real guns firing blanks. The kids in the crowd especially love it.

I head in the direction of the casinos. I eat at a local bar and strike up conversations with others passing through. When the sun goes down, every family in town is setting off their own fireworks. The atmosphere is one of excitement. Blasts and bangs are all around me. The smell of gunpowder wafts through the night. Closing my eyes, these mix with scenes from old westerns, and for a moment, it could be … 1880.

The midday sun is hot. Cement sculptures of Adam and Eve greet me at the entrance of what is known as the Garden of Eden in the small town of Lucas, Kansas. Inside the fenced-in yard, 40-foot-tall cement trees hold clusters of sculptures depicting larger-than-life biblical, political, and historical scenes. An angel flies overhead. The devil lurks with red, glowing eyes. There are men, women, and children. There are animals: a dog, a fox, a bird eating a worm, and an octopus. The crucifixion is represented, but it is "Labor" nailed to the cross.

Samuel Perry Dinsmoor created this sculpture garden in the yard surrounding his home to express his political and religious views. The Civil War veteran and eccentric artist began working on his creation in 1907 at the age of 62. Despite his bad eyesight, he continued working on it for more than 20 years, stopping not because he was finished, but because he'd gone blind.

His Garden of Eden made him unpopular with his neighbors. Most of them found the images disturbing and, well, kind of creepy. While I am impressed with his accomplishment and dedication, I can see why his neighbors were less than thrilled. There is something unsettling about it. Not only the bold, powerful images, but the bizarre faces and shapes. Maybe it is because they are made from cement ... and suspended overhead.

Dinsmoor didn't seem to mind his unpopularity and was no stranger to scandal. For example, he married his second wife when she was already pregnant with the first of their two (some reports say four) children. He was 81. She was 20.

He fully intended his sculpture garden to be opened to the public after his death. Today, tourists can even visit his tomb at the corner of the yard and are invited to look into the face of Dinsmoor himself through a glass-covered casket.

DINSMOOR, HIS SECOND WIFE AND ONE OF THEIR CHILDREN

By the end of the weekend, I am back in Wichita walking among the old buildings and brick-lined streets. The town is clean and the people are friendly. There are lots of choices for good food and the prices—compared to DC—are fantastic.

I stop in at Mort's Martini and Cigar Bar for a drink and live music. The band does a superb cover of Bob Marley's "Stir It Up" as the images of the day flash across my mind.

CALL OF THE DRAGON

It's 3:00 in the morning. I'm staring at the ceiling, wide awake. This is not a rare occurrence. Even as a child, I had trouble sleeping at night. I'd wait until my parents fell asleep and sneak downstairs to watch television or quietly play with my toys. This was cool then. It was like a superpower. I didn't need to sleep like regular kids. As an adult, however, it's not so special. Things like going to work and meeting deadlines on no sleep spoil the fun, and afternoon naps are harder to squeeze in.

Anyway, it's one of those nights. My mind is a circus of random thoughts and I know I'm not going to sleep. An article I read recently about a road on the border of North Carolina and Tennessee whips to the front of my mind. Motorcyclists refer to it as the "Tail of the Dragon" because the 11-mile stretch boasts 318 curves and dares bikers from far and wide to test their skills.

Since I can't sleep and tomorrow kicks off a three-day weekend, I could ...

"Absolutely not!" I say, aloud, trying to be rational. "It's 3:00 in the morning! If you can't sleep, you read a book or watch television like a normal person. That place has to be least 9 or 10 hours from here!"

But it's already too late for sensible arguments. I'm looking at maps on the Internet. When I realize I could take the Blue Ridge Parkway for a huge chunk of the ride, there's no turning back. I'm loading the saddlebags and adding a camera I bought recently that attaches to the bike.

By 3:30, I'm on the road. Already, there is traffic, people heading out of DC, but it's not bad and, before I know it, I'm on a byway and have it all to myself. Roaring through the Virginia countryside on a chilly October morning just before sunrise on a motorcycle is pure bliss. The sun is rising as I reach Waynesboro where I stop for breakfast before getting on the Blue Ridge Parkway. Gloriously hot coffee helps shake off the chill before I head for the parkway after figuring out how and where to attach the camera to the bike.

The first 10 or 12 pictures I take look like this:

UNINTENTIONAL SELFIE

The Blue Ridge Parkway is almost 500 miles of mountains and scenic beauty; it is said to be one of the most gorgeous rides in America. No argument here. Once I figure the camera out, I get these:

NOW THE CAMERA IS WORKING

BLUE RIDGE PARKWAY

At the Visitor Center, a very helpful but rather stern woman gives me some tips. "There's no gas on the parkway," she snaps. "You can't just stop when your tank is low. You have to plan ahead."

She comes to my side of the counter and spreads a map out in front of me. "There are only certain places where you can get off to fuel up. You try taking a random side road, and you'll end up lost."

"I have a GPS that—"

"Put it away," she says. "They don't work down here. People get lost all the time relying on those things. You follow the map and the mile markers." She reminds me of Mickey, the salty trainer brilliantly played by Burgess Meredith in the *Rocky* movies: harsh, in your face, unapologetic, and yet, impossible not to like. "Once you get off at these designated places, you will be anywhere from one to eight miles from a gas station, so don't cut it close. Play it safe. Get gas before you are low."

I make a note of this because playing it safe has never been my strong suit.

"How far are you going?"

"Not sure." Her expression tells me this is the wrong answer. "Probably the whole way."

"It's getting late. You're on a motorcycle, traveling alone, am I right?"

"Exactly."

"If you're smart, you stop for the night."

"Yeah, I was thinking I'd stop in Roanoke."

She nods her approval. "That's a good 90 minutes from here. You know there's rain coming, right?"

"Yes, ma'am, but I should be in Roanoke long before it hits."

"Should be," she says, cocking an eyebrow, "but you never know. Weather forecasters are about as accurate down here as your GPS."

Back on the road, the ride is amazing, but less than a half-hour after leaving the visitor center, dark clouds roll in. I am a good 60 miles from Roanoke when the sky opens up and the rain pours. In a few minutes, I'm cold and soaked to the bone, but this is the least of my concerns. I can barely see the road through a foggy, rain-blurred visor. Wet brakes don't respond well, and the turns that were so much fun earlier are now treacherous.

I take the first outlet I see off the parkway. I'm still 20 miles away from the nearest town, but that beats being 60 miles away.

After reserving a room at the only motel in a small town I've already forgotten the name of, I jog to the Food Lion across the street for something to microwave because once I get out of these wet clothes, I am not going to want to get back into them anytime soon. Just as I find the soup aisle, a woman pushing a grocery cart and surrounded by a gaggle of young children says to me, "Why bless your heart, riding a motorcycle in the pouring rain. My, my."

I work with a couple of Southern women and that's a polite way of calling someone an idiot without actually calling them an idiot. I am in no mood, but I smile and shrug.

Smirking and shaking her head, she says, "Bless your little heart."

"Nice hat."

Her hand self-consciously goes to her yellow rain hat. She starts to say something—probably, "What's wrong with my hat?"—but then rolls her eyes and moves on.

Actually, there is nothing at all wrong with her hat, but she will probably spend the next good while wondering why I said that. *Bless her heart! Bless her little heart.*

No trouble sleeping last night. The sun is out and the day is clear and warm. I take my time, enjoy the ride, stop at the overlooks, and take a short hike. I am surprised to see how many people are alone. Some on motorcycles, others in cars, they stop to gaze out over the mountains and breathe it all in. "I never get sick of looking at it," the guy next to me at the Thunder Hill overlook says, almost to himself.

"Where are you heading?" I ask, assuming he is on a trip.

"Work," he says. "I live nearby. Make it a point to get up every so often."

This reminds me of the year I lived on the east end of Long Island, New York. People would drive to the edge of the beach in the early mornings and watch the ocean waves for a few minutes before getting on with their day.

It gives me hope when I see people do this because the desire to seek nature and the ability to appreciate it has to come from a good place.

As the sun starts to set, I pull into a small North Carolina town with two motels, a gas station, a chapel, and two bars, all clumped together right off the exit. I get a room, shower off the road, and look at the map. I have drifted farther south than I intended and need to start heading northwest tomorrow morning if I want to ride the Dragon in Deal's Gap.

The bar I walk to for dinner has a bartender who calls everyone "honey" and takes pride in knowing what her regulars drink and how they like their burgers. I ask her if there is a downtown area to explore later.

She laughs and says in a southern drawl, "You're in it, honey. This is all we got."

"That's fine. Beautiful country around here."

"Why thank you. Lived here my whole life. Couldn't pay me to live anywhere else."

She sells me on the barbecue bacon burger and I order a cold beer to go with it. I figure I am about 3 ½ hours from the Dragon. I could sleep in tomorrow and still be there by early afternoon.

But there's a problem. The Weather Channel is telling a completely different story than it told yesterday. It is raining in Deal's Gap at the moment and that rain is now supposed to continue off and on for the next several days.

Do I stick to the plan tomorrow morning or call it off and head for home?

I have always been a "cross-the-finish-line-no-matter-what" kind of guy and that is my impulse now. *I said I was going to ride the Dragon, and by God, that's exactly what I am going to do!*

However, after enjoying a delicious burger and the gentle buzz of a third beer, I am more reflective. *What's the point in going there if it's raining? Even if it stops for a period, what fun will those 318 curves be on wet roads? Going there just because you told yourself you were going to do it doesn't make a lot of sense, does it?*

No. It doesn't.

In my defense, the impulse to reach the destination regardless of the circumstances exists in me for a good reason. I had to fight hard for the opportunities I've had in my life, and it was that stick-to-itiveness that drove me forward when the road ahead was blocked around every turn. Back then, it seemed the adage about the journey being more important than the destination was backwards.

Even though my compulsion to go forward through hell and high water will always be a part of me, I have learned over many years of successes and failures that it really is the journey that matters most. Success—regardless of hard work, talent, or determination—is never guaranteed. The journey, however, is a sure thing.

So...while the call of the Dragon will have to go unanswered for now, the Virginia countryside at dawn, the gorgeous ride on the Blue Ridge Parkway, the people I talked to, the food I ate, and even the frustration of getting caught in a downpour are all mine to keep.

But this is not a forfeit, Dear Dragon. Oh no, it is merely a *rain check*.

I shall return one day.

GREENLIGHT

Tonight's accommodations are in the middle of nowhere and could provide a time capsule for the 1970s. All one-level, each of the 16 rooms of the motel has a parking space in front of an orange door. Most of those are currently occupied with an old car or a pickup. In the office, I am greeted by the owner, a heavy-set woman with no teeth, wearing a pink bathrobe over floral pajamas.

There are only two remaining rooms, she tells me, because tomorrow is the first day of squirrel season. With tax and fees, it is 46 dollars, which is about half the price I usually end up paying. She hands me an actual key instead of the card or a fob that I'm used to.

"There'll be hot coffee here in the morning, hun," she says. "It will be ready by 6:00 and you're entitled to as many free cups as you can drink until 10:00."

"That sounds great. Thank you."

"I put out a box of powdered doughnuts too, but they go quick. First come, first served."

My room is dank and musty smelling and the furniture is older than I am. The curtains are stained yellow by cigarette smoke from years gone by. A noisy hot water tank is behind the closet door. The bedspread is thin and faded. The sheets beneath it are bleached within an inch of their lives. But at least they are clean and the warmth of the room is nice after the chilly ride here. The hot shower feels fantastic.

I have no phone reception, but the Wi-Fi signal is surprisingly strong and comes free with the room. I open a bottle of wine that I picked up earlier this afternoon and drink it from a paper cup as I fire up my laptop and start writing a story about a group of guys who get together at an old motel in West Virginia for the first day of squirrel hunting.

It's a bright, beautiful morning. The air is crisp and clean, though colder than I'd hoped. Fortunately, I prepared for the possibility with extra clothes. The powdered doughnuts are long gone, but I enjoy a cup of coffee on the front steps of the motel office and, after spotting a loaded apple tree, I have fresh fruit for breakfast.

I head south-west ... just because. After an hour of twisty mountain roads, I find myself sitting at the only traffic light in a small, West Virginia town. I'm thinking about my Aunt Jan. She passed away a couple of years ago, but memories of her always make me smile. She lived most of her adult life in this area of West Virginia and spoke with a southern twang that we kids back in Pennsylvania always got a kick out of hearing.

I grew up in a one-traffic-light town and I remember sitting at it when I was a fifteen-year-old boy with a learner's permit. My mom was in the passenger's seat and Aunt Jan was in the back. It is hard to look cool cruising with your mother and your aunt, but they had errands to run, offered to let me drive, and I needed all the practice I could get.

We had a Dodge Charger. It was a stick shift and I loved driving it, but I still had problems taking off. We came to that stoplight and damn if it didn't turn red just as I got to it. To make matters worse, there was a group of tough guys—all older than me—hanging out at the corner gas station. I was pretending not to notice them and silently praying I could take off without any problems.

The light turned green and I stalled right in the middle of the intersection. As if on cue, the guys at the gas station started cheering and clapping and laughing. My face was on fire. In a panic, I started the car and stalled again, which really got them going. This was a fifteen-year-old boy's nightmare. Before the light turned red again, I managed to jerk and grind my way out of the interaction and down Main Street. As soon as we got out of town, I pulled off. "Forget it," I said, dramatically jumping out of the vehicle. "I hate this car. I'll never be able to drive it."

Once my mom and Jan realized that I was not getting behind the wheel again, Jan took over and I climbed in back, sulking, hating myself. Of course, they told me I was being ridiculous. The only way to learn a thing was to do it and failing at it was just a part of the process. But that was all lost on me. I wasn't listening. I was convinced I was a loser, my life sucked, and I would forever walk under a cloud of shame.

By the time the errands were completed and we got back to town, it was dark. "Take the side streets," I said from the backseat. Jan ignored me. She drove right down Main Street and stopped at the red light again. The guys were still there and started hooting and hollering as soon as they saw the Charger. "Encore!" one of them shouted. "Encore!"

If I could have crawled under the seat and died, I would have. Jan egged them on by revving the engine.

"Come on, Aunt Jan!" I pleaded. "Don't!"

She looked at me in the rearview mirror, all smiles, and said in her southern drawl, "Honey, them old boys can't see in here at night. They don't know it's your fat, old Aunt Jan behind the wheel. They think it's you."

The light turned green and Jan peeled out, squealing the tires the whole way through the intersection. That was the very last thing those guys were expecting. They all stood there, stupefied, mouths agape, as we roared out of town.

Jan and Mom were laughing and doing a little hooting and hollering themselves at that point and I couldn't help joining in. When we were out of town, Jan pulled over and still giggling said to me, "Next time, it's gonna be you behind the wheel. So, get your little ass up here and learn how to drive this thing!"

There's no one around as I sit here today, but when the light turns green, I do my Aunt Jan proud ...and lay a little rubber.

A PROPER GOODBYE

This is the part where I am supposed to ride off into the sunset. For almost two years, I have been saving, planning, and working for this moment. The motorcycle is packed for an open-ended road trip. Everything else I own is in storage. As of tomorrow, my apartment is no longer my apartment and, already, some other guy is sitting in my cubicle at the office. I have done what I set out to do. The time has arrived.

But something doesn't feel right. Something is missing.

Am I having second thoughts? Getting cold feet? I sure hope not. It's a little late for that. There is no turning back now.

Walking helps me think so I start wandering through Westover Village, the neighborhood in Arlington, Virginia I have called home for the past five years.

It's perfect walking weather. Mid-afternoon, early October. Sunny and warm, but not hot. A breeze moves through the trees that line the streets, their leaves newly turned red and yellow and orange. "I wish I had your guts!" my boss said to me last week. It was a sentiment I heard repeatedly at the surprise farewell lunch they had for me in the breakroom. Most were excited for me. A few looked at me like I was out of my mind. Is it guts, I wonder, or is it madness to leave the best paying job I've ever had for the unknown, living on savings for a year and not knowing how I will reenter the workforce when the time and money are gone?

"If you ever change your mind," my boss said, between bites of cake decorated with a winding road and a little plastic motorcycle, "we'll be glad to take you back. Of course, you won't need us when you are on the bestseller list."

She is sincere, I know, but things change fast in DC. She will be on a different contract a year from now, maybe even with a different company. And how a book—any book, regardless of merit or style—becomes a bestseller is one of life's great mysteries.

No, I am under no illusions about the gravity of the risk I am taking.

I cut through the park and pick up the Custis Trail, a narrow, concrete bike lane that runs under I-66. Cyclists and joggers abound. "On your left!" they say when approaching from behind. I smile at a memory from the first time I walked this route five years ago. My mind was lost in the novel I was trying to finish. Someone shouted, "Left!"

Unfamiliar with walking on bike trails at the time, I instinctually turned to my left, which, of course, put me directly into their path. I still don't know how we avoided a collision, but we did.

Images from the countless miles I have tramped on these trails and the streets of northern Virginia and Washington, DC flood my mind. I like to walk in all seasons and will go in any weather. I even trekked through "Snowmaggedon"—one of the worst blizzards in the area's history—during my first winter here in 2010. The snow poured from the night sky, blurring the city lights. The next morning, nearly two feet of it was on the ground and trees drooped under the excessive weight. An eerie silence had fallen over the entire region. Cars were buried, roads and sidewalks had disappeared. No distant clanging of the Metro. No buses. No cars or trucks.

The trail comes out in Ballston and, from there, I walk the streets on into Clarendon as the last golden rays of sun intensify. All the swanky places have patios full of good-looking people in their casual, yet classy fall clothes, wearing designer shades, laughing over sparkling glasses of good wine, colorful martinis, margaritas, mimosas, and mugs of craft beer. The smells of baking bread, onions,

garlic, steak, chicken, and fish drift through the air from a dozen restaurants featuring a variety of cuisines from different cultures.

I never considered myself to be one these hipsters, but I did get to know a lot of them during my time here. These late afternoon meetups are the reward for fighting through high-pressured jobs and confining cubicles. The bars and restaurants here are expensive, but this crowd can afford it. Mostly, they are groups of friends and co-workers meeting for happy hours that will go on well into the evening. I also recognize couples meeting from dating sites, trying not to get their hopes up while secretly praying they meet the person that will finally save their lonely soul. Too, there are people rediscovering their significant others and giving themselves some well-earned credit for making it or at least staying in the game in this very competitive, mad, fast-paced region of the country.

I have sat at many of these tables and been in all of those situations with endless combinations of friends, co-workers, and girlfriends over the past five years, eating whatever the latest happy hour specials happened to be—raw oysters, steamed mussels, bruschetta, imported olives and cheeses—while getting drunk on Belgian beers, sangria, or shots of whiskey.

I don't see a single familiar face as I drift by tonight like the stranger I will soon become here, and suddenly, I know what was missing earlier. While I took the time to say goodbye to friends, acquaintances, co-workers, and neighbors, I'd forgotten to say goodbye to the places themselves.

Which, I guess, is what I'm doing now.

Stopping at my favorite Japanese restaurant, I sit down to a feast of fresh sushi and raise a glass to Arlington and DC. Though I am glad to be leaving, I am going to miss you and will always appreciate my time here. So, goodbye and farewell.

Now ... I have a sunset to ride off into!

TAKING THE LONG WAY HOME

I have been meandering southern and central Virginia for the past two days. This is the point I would normally have to turn the motorcycle around and make a beeline home to make it to work on time. As much as I loved those weekend trips, they ended too quickly. Gazing west or south, I resented the fact that I couldn't keep going.

But not today. Today, tomorrow, and for months to come, I have no schedule, no deadlines, and absolutely no place I have to be. For two years, I saved and planned to have no plan. And here I am, whipping across the open road, high on the smell of forests and grape orchards baking in the autumn sun.

So, what now? Ride west or south until I reach a warmer climate?

That's what I always assumed I'd do if I had the chance, but instead, something is pulling me north to Pennsylvania for a place I can land near my family and get to work on the new book. Out here on the road, the characters I imagine returning for the sequel of *Strip Cuts*, my first novel, are flooding my mind, whispering in my ear, demanding that I settle in somewhere and start writing their stories.

North it is, but still, I'm taking my good old time.

When I see a sign for Rockville, Maryland, I take a detour. If memory serves, that is where F. Scott Fitzgerald is buried. I discovered his work at the community college in Pittsburgh and rediscovered it at the University of Iowa where I got my Masters. Few writers can pack as much into a single line as Fitzgerald, but in truth, I was just as fascinated with his life as his work. He not only captured the Roaring 20s in his writing, he lived it with his equally brilliant wife, Zelda. Their love affair was wild, romantic, reckless, and ultimately, tragic.

The cemetery is small. Easy to miss.

He and Zelda are buried side by side. At first, it appears the grave has been trashed, but upon closer inspection, I realize the clutter is made up of objects left to pay homage: coins, a pen, a poem, cut flowers, and a note. Someone apparently sat here and drank a beer with Mr. and Mrs. Fitzgerald. (Though gin would have been more appropriate; Gin Rickey was their drink of choice.)

I kneel next to the final resting place of the once fun-loving, carefree couple, living symbols of the Roaring 20s and recall the narrator of his most famous novel, *The Great Gatsby*, commenting on "the inexhaustible variety of life" and how it "simultaneously enchanted and repelled" him.

I feel a little sad thinking of how their lives ended. Scott, his body ravaged by alcoholism, died at only 44; Zelda spent the last years of her life in a mental hospital and tragically died in a fire there.

I run my hand along the cold stone where the famous last line of *Gatsby* is engraved: "So we beat on, boats against the current, borne back ceaselessly into the past."

Keeping with the theme of the day, I head to Baltimore where Edgar Allan Poe is buried. I stand in front of a parking kiosk trying to get it to take my money. I can feel someone standing behind me, waiting, so I start pushing the button repeatedly as if that's going to make a difference.

"This machine is finicky," the person behind me says. "I park here every day." I turn to see an attractive woman in scrubs and tennis shoes, her hair in a loose bun on top of her head. "May I?"

"Please," I say, stepping aside.

She cancels the transaction. The machine spits out my money, she puts it back in, hits some buttons, and a few seconds later, hands me my receipt. "What would you do without me?"

"Probably get a ticket," I say.

Looking at my motorcycle, she asks where I am going to put the receipt. I tell her I'll stick it under the lock cover on the gas cap.

"Couldn't someone steal it and put it on the dash of their car?"

"Easily," I say, "but, you know, no one ever has."

She takes her own receipt from the kiosk and says, "So, is there anything else I can do for you today?"

I am about to say, "You can have a drink with me later," when I spot the wedding ring. Damn. "No, I think I'm good," I say, nodding toward the cemetery. "Just stopping off to visit Edgar."

"Tell him I said hello," she says, giving me one last smile before heading off in the direction of the hospital where she works.

Standing in front of Poe's memorial, I wonder if he knows he finally got the recognition he deserved. He sure never got it in his lifetime. Originally, he was buried in the back of this cemetery. For years, he didn't even have a headstone. There was just a marker that read: 80.

His death is still a mystery. He was found on the streets, incoherent and looking disheveled, wearing ill-fitting clothes. He was taken to a hospital where he went into a coma and, never regaining consciousness, died several days later.

For years, alcohol and drugs were blamed, but it appears that suggestion was largely made-up and fueled by a spiteful critic who was jealous of Poe's talent and purposely tried to keep him from finding his place in history.

There are a wide range of other compelling theories. Some believe he was murdered. Others claim it was a disease or an illness that killed him. Everything from tuberculosis to syphilis, epilepsy to diabetes to rabies have been entertained and argued. One theory even suggests he was a victim of a voting scam called "cooping" where people were randomly kidnapped, drugged, sometimes beaten, and forced to vote in different districts for a crooked politician.

There is much written on this if you want to check it out...and believe me, Poe's death is as shadowy and creepy as the short stories he so masterfully crafted.

I wake up in a Pennsylvania motel. It's 40 degrees outside so I'm in no hurry to get back on the road. I go to the gas station across the street for coffee and doughnuts. Checkout is a few hours away, which should give the temperature time to go up another 10 or 12 degrees. Still, a chilly ride, but doable.

In the meantime, I'll enjoy the warmth of the room and revisit some of the places this long ride home has taken me.

BARBOURSVILLE, VA

HANGING OUT IN WV

WHILE I'M FAIRLY CERTAIN THIS WAS NEVER GEORGE WASHINGTON'S BATHTUB, THE FATHER OF OUR COUNTRY DID INDEED VISIT WHAT IS NOW BERKLEY SPRINGS, WEST VIRGINIA.

ORIGINALLY BUILT IN BEDFORD, PENNSYLVANIA IN 1927, THIS UNUSUAL BUILDING WAS ONCE A RESTAURANT WHICH USED TO SERVE LUNCH, ICE CREAM, AND OF COURSE, COFFEE.

WAYWARD SON: TRAVELS AND REFLECTIONS

A GOOD BAR

The second thing I do when I settle into a new area is look for a good bar. (The first is to get a library card, but that is quick and easy.) Finding a watering hole I will want to frequent takes some time. There is no shortage of them around, and since consistency is one of the qualities I'm looking for, I will visit a few times before I make my choice. That doesn't mean I won't go to the others; it simply means that I will have a go-to place that I can count on, a place where—as the 80s sitcom *Cheers* once touted—"everybody knows your name."

To an extent, what constitutes a good bar depends on who you are and specifically what you're looking for. You wouldn't expect the same thing from a classy wine or cigar bar that you would from a pub or a dive. Since I am now living in western Pennsylvania and writing for a local paper, my interest is local. However, having lived in big cities and small towns all over the United States and visited more than a handful of European countries, I will say that there are certain merits that transcend class, locale, and culture. Whether you're wearing a sports jacket and sipping a fine Scotch or enjoying a mug of beer while dressed in jeans and a sweatshirt, there are things that I believe are universal in the making of a good bar.

Local color is always an appealing characteristic in a bar, and as a writer, I find it especially significant. The clientele says something about the people who live and work in that particular corner of the world. Recently, for example, I was in a place where a guy had had too much to drink and his wife came to take him home. She was not pleased and he was nowhere near ready to leave when she arrived. It was an embarrassing situation for the couple that had the potential to turn ugly, but the bartender and the other patrons kept the guy talking and laughing while communicating with his wife through silent nods and winks. In about 15 minutes or so, they'd defused the situation and subtly steered him into her care and out the door. After they left, I found out that the couple were regulars and going through a difficult period in their lives. There were no snide remarks and a few minutes later, the subject was dropped altogether.

Another given in a good bar, of course, is that they have or—in the case of a small town—are willing to stock your favorite drink provided you come in somewhat regularly to order it. Good food and cleanliness are also vital. However, none of that will matter much if the establishment does not offer reliable service and a friendly, welcoming environment. And the key to that—the special ingredient that makes the drink, so to speak—is a good bartender.

He or she never forgets that they are the host and everyone that walks through the door is a guest. Over the years, some have made a lasting impression on me. "I try to keep a positive attitude," one of my favorite bartenders once told me of her trade, "and greet everyone that comes in with a smile. Even if it's a Friday or Saturday night and I am in the weeds, I at least acknowledge them and let them know I will be with them as soon as possible."

She worked in California's San Fernando Valley and I remember how she would, when appropriate, introduce guests who have similar interests to each other or, if a discussion was going on among a couple of patrons, she'd invite someone who was listening in but was too shy or socially awkward to know how to enter the conversation.

In other words, she understood that nobody goes to a bar just to drink. Even if they don't admit it, are not overly sociable, or particularly talkative, they go for the company and to be around other people. Even the curmudgeon who proudly proclaims to "hate people" is there to be around them, though it may be merely to gather more material to complain about.

Speaking of curmudgeons, when I told a grizzled, old fellow what I was up to a few days ago, he laughed. "You ain't gonna find nothing like that around here."

"I'm not so sure about that," I told him. "I have already found a possible contender or two."

He waved me off. "I'd rather go to a dump with bad service anyway."

I had to ask. "Why is that?"

"Don't have to tip."

I filed that comment away in a mental folder labeled "Dumb Things People Say" and wished him all the bad service and dumpy bars he could stand.

As for me, the search continues.

WAYWARD SON: TRAVELS AND REFLECTIONS

NATURAL INSPIRATION

I was so desperate for motivation last week, I Googled it.

I'm not kidding. I was in a rut. Maybe it was the effect of this long, cold winter or perhaps it was just a few too many frustrating events in a row. Who knows? At first, I let it ride, telling myself that it was okay to feel a little blue. And it is. It's a normal part of life. We're not built to be happy all the time. But we're not built to mope around on the couch all the time either, which is what I was doing.

Thankfully, a small internal voice had had enough and cried out, "Seriously, dude, this is getting ridiculous. You have a to-do list a mile long and you are supposed to be starting the next book. You need to get moving, find some motivation." The best I could manage at that point was a Google search.

On the subject of motivation, I read the opinions and thoughts of great minds—Ralph Waldo Emerson, Albert Einstein, Taylor Swift ("Shake it off, shake it off, oh, oh!")—and started to feel a little more lively. Then I read this simple statement by the naturalist, John Muir: "Between every two pines is a doorway to a new world."

Bam! That did it. Before I could talk myself out of it, I was off the couch and going for my hiking boots. Why didn't I think of that before? A hike in the woods has always been my cure-all. It didn't matter that it was cold out or that the ground was covered in snow. Trekking through nature always gave me a lift, regardless of the season.

One of the best things about being back in Clarion County is that no matter which direction I go, I am never more than a few minutes from the woods. Generally, when I want a great place to hike, I go to the old train lines reborn as Rails to Trails, but that day, I wanted the woods where I grew up. I drove to my parent's house, thinking I'd get Dad to join me as he is always up for a hike. However, the pickup was gone when I got there and he and Mom were out and about. I parked in their driveway and tramped up through the yard and into the woods as I've done since I was a little kid.

The cold air was jarring at first. To get my blood moving, I walked at a good pace, my boots crunching through the wooded hillside and out across an open field. Once I was warm, I enjoyed the crisp air and started to appreciate my surroundings: the pale-blue sky, how the sunlight filtered through the bare trees and sparkled off the thin layer of snow. I walked across the strip cuts and stopped at the edge of a spoil pile to take in the view of the river below and mile after mile of tree-covered hills. I remembered going to that spot as a teenager when I felt stifled or trapped, afraid that the big dreams I was bursting with would never come true. Sitting up there always made me feel better. It put everything into perspective, made the world appear almost manageable, something a person could navigate if they put their mind to it.

Back into the forest then, I walked for another hour, angling so I would travel in a huge circle that would eventually end up back where I started. I came to a wall of giant pine trees, thick and close together. The John Muir line that got me off of the couch came to mind as I walked into the pines. It felt like stepping into an old church, calm and sacred. The snow never made it through the thick branches of the evergreens so the ground was dry and covered with a carpet of soft brown needles. I sat cross-legged and gazed up at the bits of blue sky visible between the treetops. I stayed there for a long while, soaking up the silence, thinking of all the places I've traveled, the many jobs I've held, the things I've done, and the people who have moved in and out of my life.

And, too, I thought about the future. What's next? What now?

When it got too cold to sit, I started moving again. By the time I saw the house I grew up in on the horizon, I was fully charged, reconnected to myself and the land. The old Ford was back in the driveway and, feeling so much better than I had that morning, I decided to stop in for a cup of coffee with Mom and Dad.

There is still plenty of winter left so if you find yourself feeling blue or burning with cabin fever, remember the ample forests of western Pennsylvania are open all year round, free, and offer the "doorway to a different world."

If that doesn't get you off the couch, try Googling "inspiration."

LOVE BITES

Romance is going to the dogs. Literally.

I like dogs and they tend to like me too, but they are at the center of a disturbing trend that is seriously cramping my style. Every woman I have gone out with during the past few years has had a big dog in her life that made dating very difficult. I could tell you dozens of stories, but in the interest of time, I will only tell you the most recent one just before leaving the DC Metro Area. Krissy (not her real name) and I met at the party of a mutual friend. She was smart, attractive, and we had some things in common. I asked her out and things were going great until I met the other important male in her life: Booger.

Right off, I didn't like his name, but that wasn't his fault. He was a huge, hairy mutt who loved everyone—except other dogs that he tried to kill—and he absolutely adored Krissy, who absolutely adored him right back.

Krissy and I lasted three months.

Our final day together was a sunny Saturday this past October. We'd planned a walk around the city and I'd arrived at her place with a bouquet of sunflowers. I anticipated us strolling around Old Town, hand in hand, talking and laughing easily, stopping at a little café, browsing novelty shops, going wherever the day took us.

While Krissy put the flowers in a vase, I loaded the fireplace with wood for later that evening. I joined her in the kitchen and was about to kiss her when she yelled, "Booger! Wanna go walkie? Booger wanna walkie?"

There was a thundering sound from the far end of the house as the 90-pound dog raced through the living room and down the hall. He burst into the kitchen, skidded across the tile floor, and slammed into the table. The vase of sunflowers crashed to the floor.

Krissy is a well-educated woman with an impressive vocabulary that went out the window when Booger was around. "Bad Boogie! Bad, bad!"

The dog whimpered, ashamed, but still, it did not dampen his enthusiasm. He was overjoyed, wide-eyed, shaking with excitement. Krissy forgot about the flowers and asked, "You wanna go?"

Oh, did he ever! He began howling and spinning in circles. "Go get your leash!" she laughed, matching his excitement, shaking her head and hands wildly, making funny faces. "Go on! Go get it! Go!"

He exploded out of the kitchen, rumbling through the house as we knelt to clean up the mess. She looked at me, narrowed her eyes, and said, "What's the matter?"

"Nothing. I was picturing," I stammered, "a romantic walk...you know...just the two of us."

Booger tore back into the kitchen, sliding across the floor again, panting and drooling, the leash clutched tightly in his mouth. With his tail going uncontrollably, he looked at us as if we were the most wonderful human beings on the planet and he was the luckiest dog ever.

Still on our knees, we were eye level with Booger and Krissy said to him in a deeply disappointed voice, "Boogie stay home. No walk-ie." The dog's eyebrows twitched up and down like he didn't understand and the manic wagging of his tail began to slow. "No walkie. No!"

A whine escaped the dog and the leash fell from his mouth with a heartbreaking clatter.

I couldn't take it. "No," I said. "He can go. Of course, he can go."

She glared at me. "You say that now, but you'll act all weird on the walk."

"No," I said, "I promise. He can go. I want him to go. Really."

She turned to Booger then and whispered, "You wanna go?"

The romantic walk I'd envisioned was doomed. With Booger tangling his leash around everything imaginable and continually jerking Krissy forward, it was impossible for us to carry on a conversation or even hold hands. The café and novelty shops were out too because Booger suffered from separation anxiety and couldn't be left alone outside. The beginning of the end came when she was cleaning up after him and he took the opportunity to break free and attack another big dog being walked by another pretty woman.

Krissy screamed, handed me the baggie she'd just filled, and ran after her beloved dog. She and the other woman managed to get the dogs separated, after which they exchanged unpleasantries, each blaming the other's dog for the scuffle. When Krissy stormed back, she said I was acting weird like she knew I would. I denied this and we got into an argument right there. She informed me that she and Booger were going home alone and my invitation to spend the night was revoked.

Watching them walk away while I stood there holding a bag of doggie waste, I imagined them cuddled up in front of the fire I'd prepared and knew I couldn't compete with Booger. His schedule was completely in sync with hers. They never quarreled. He was ecstatic every time she walked through the door, was never grumpy, and he was trainable. Sure, he'd misbehave from time to time, but he'd be very ashamed of it, and his transgressions would never involve stealing a glance at another woman or staying out too late with the guys.

And doggone it, I couldn't even be angry at him.

FAMILIAR FACES

Seeing the same people everywhere you go is one of the aspects of small town living I forgot all about and one that I am trying to readjust to since moving back to my hometown. I see the librarian at the gas station, the mailman at the coffee shop, my next-door neighbor at the diner, the waitress at the gym, and I will eventually run into all of them again—and practically everyone else I know—at Walmart.

After years of living in the city, one gets used to a certain level of anonymity. If you're feeling unsociable or go out looking like a slob, it's no big deal. Unless you are flat out rude or dressed in rags, no one will notice, and even if they do, odds are, they'll never see you again.

But it's different in a small town. Being unsociable will get you labeled as "uppity" or "thinking you're better than," and the minute you go to town looking like a bum, you're bound to run into your old high school sweetheart or the teacher who said you'd never amount to anything. In a small town, like it or not, you're part of a community. People know you and hold you accountable for your actions.

Recently, I made plans to meet an old friend for a drink (after running into him at Walmart, of course). "Do you mind coming by and picking me up?" he asked.

"Not at all. Are you having car problems?"

"No. I don't want anyone to see my truck sitting at the bar."

I gave him a blank stare. "You're kidding."

"No, man," he said, then lowered his voice and added, "I started teaching a Sunday School class. I can't be seen hanging at the bar."

"We are having a beer or two," I said, "not going on a bender and terrorizing the town. And if it's such a big deal, what about people seeing my car there?"

"You're a writer. No one will be surprised."

Real nice. Thanks, buddy.

Regardless of whether you live in a city or a small town, people are naturally voyeuristic to a certain extent. How else would you explain the fascination with reality shows, the tabloids, and Facebook? It's just that, in a small town, as Miranda Lambert notes in one of her hit songs: "Every...rural heart's got a story to tell, every grandma, in-law, ex-girlfriend, maybe knows you just a little too well."

But it's not all bad. On a planet with over seven billion inhabitants, it is easy to feel insignificant, just another number among billions of numbers, so there is a kind of reassurance in seeing familiar faces everywhere you go, having someone to ask about your family or join you in griping about the weather.

Living in the big cities, the first thing people ask upon meeting you is, "What do you do?" And so that's their point of reference, it's who you are—a lawyer, a janitor, a truck driver—and probably all you will ever be to them. In a small town, people know a job is just how you pay the bills. They are much more interested in how many fish you caught last week, what kind of garden you're putting in, if you're still volunteering at the high school, or running in the 5K at this year's Peanut Butter Festival. While it may be a little annoying that everyone knows you got a speeding ticket the other day, at least they think of you as a unique individual and not just another number.

Also, if your car happens to break down or you run out of gas on a busy freeway or a city street, good luck. The only thing other drivers will be concerned about is that you get that car to the side of the road and out of their way. In a small town, someone will almost certainly stop and help you get moving again. After all, they can hardly leave you stranded on the side of the road when they know full well they are going to see you next week at the Riverside or the high school play.

Aside from these benefits, I've noticed that those living in rural areas seem to have a bit of an edge over city slickers when it comes to mastering one of life's greatest challenges: accepting yourself for who you are, and being comfortable in your own skin. Maybe it's the lack of anonymity, being a visible part of the community, or simply not getting lost in the fast pace of the city, but that self-awareness—even if it's forced on you by your surroundings—can be an advantage.

Plus, it can be rather comforting to run into a familiar face at Walmart and gripe about the weather.

VISITING

How would you like to peek through a window into the past? Relive some of your favorite memories from growing up? Reconnect with the people, places, and experiences that formed you, maybe even hear some family secrets, and get a glimpse of what the world was like before you were born?

You can, and it's easier than you think: Go visiting. Spend an afternoon or an evening with aunts and uncles you haven't seen in forever, grandparents (if you're lucky enough to still have them), long lost cousins, and old friends.

I've been doing this since I came back to the area and hope to do a lot more in the coming months. I like to call ahead when visiting, particularly when it has been many years since I've seen the people I'm going to see. Others, however, like to just drop in. "That's how I do it with my family," my brother-in-law said. "They love it. Especially the older ones. That's the way it was done back in their day."

Visiting—as a regular pastime—was already out of fashion when I was growing up so I don't have many memories of it, but my dad tells me that this is how it was when he was a kid. "Oh yeah, friends and family would just drop in out of the blue. It wasn't a special occasion. It was normal. Mom would put on coffee and everyone would sit on the porch or around the kitchen table and talk and laugh."

I'm not sure why people stopped doing this or why it has never made a comeback. Have our lives gotten that much busier? Does scanning your wall on Facebook replace the need for face to face communication? Or is it a cultural shift, and everyone is too overscheduled for this kind of socializing and would rather unwind by watching television?

I honestly don't know. Even though visiting was something I'd intended to do when coming back to western Pennsylvania, I have to admit, it didn't come naturally to me. My sisters—who usually accompany me on visits—had to give me a little shove. And I'm glad they did. Everyone we've called on so far has been gracious, inviting, and happy for the visit.

What amazed me the most was how easy it was to reconnect with people I'd not seen for a long time—in some cases—for decades. I've found that there is always a touchstone or two you have with whomever you are visiting, a shared memory or particular time period and that's all you need. The next thing you know, you're catching each other up on the intervening years, the distance is gone, and stories are filling the air.

This is especially interesting with older folks. They remember events and relatives that you do not, and even for the ones you do remember, they will have different memories and perspectives. You will hear some great family tales and almost certainly find out some things you never knew, like who used to dig graves for a living, who kept a jug of moonshine stashed in the shed, and who the hopeless romantic was. You might discover that you're not the first one in the family with an interest in music or that your green thumb was inherited from a great aunt. The older generations will recall things about you as a child that you were too young to remember. Like an imaginary friend that you used to tell everyone about when you were four years old. It is educational, for sure, but more than that, it is fun.

It's the good times that seem to rise to the top at these gatherings and the best stories are usually the funny ones. Like the time your uncles drove a particularly frisky cat to the vet without the aid of a carrier or the time your cousin took off on a horse without first learning how to make it turn or stop.

And then there's the food, which is always an important part of these get-togethers. At most gatherings, people will want to feed you. In no time, you're reminiscing about Grandma's homemade bread, Grandpa's candied popcorn, your aunt's icebox cookies, mom's devil dogs, dad's deer jerky, and it goes on and on. When you remember these things, you want to make sure to get the recipes. Trust me, someone in your family has them. And when you get them, put them to use! Then pass the recipes on to your own kids and grandkids. They will thank you someday.

Visiting, however, is more than a trip down memory lane. Knowing something about your heritage and hearing stories of your ancestors will ground you more firmly in where you are now and where you might be heading next.

Any way you slice it, I think you'll find this is a great way to spend an evening!

SIS FLIP
Slouch
BOY
BLOOD BUCK
CHUCKLES
EGGHEAD
PUNCH Red
BUB
PINHEAD T-BONE

NICKNAMES

Listening to my aunt and uncle tell stories last weekend about people with names like Toughie, Cow Hat, and Slouch reminded me of the fascination I've always had with nicknames. My family is big on them. In fact, in the acknowledgements section of my latest novel, when I thanked my family for their support, I used my nicknames for them: Flip, Buck, Sis, Bubble, Blood, Boy, and Chuckles. I've had an attraction to such monikers for as long as I can remember. They eventually made it into my writing and continue to hold my interest.

As a little boy, I remember eavesdropping on adult conversations and being impressed by some of the names. I didn't understand the concept of nicknames at that point and thought these were the names people were born with. My young mind was reeling at the thought of how cool or tough a person had to be to have been christened T-Bone, Punch, Bear, or Chain Saw at birth.

When I got a little older and understood that these were not real names, I was even more intrigued because that meant these people somehow earned their names, sort of like the Native Americans I'd learned about in school. I soon realized, however, that nicknames were more complex than I thought. For example, I couldn't help but notice that Tiny was huge, Fatty was thin, The Giant was short, and Curly was bald.

Just when I thought I'd figured out the pattern of opposites, I'd reached the age where my peers were starting to give each other nicknames. In these cases, however, the names were not opposite, but quite literal. The redheaded kid was Red, the fastest runner in gym class was Speedy, and I won't get into the cruel nicknames, which at that age, were ruthless and made up the vast majority of them.

Though I did eventually figure out the mystery of nicknaming, my interest in the concept only continued to grow. I found out that nicknames have a long history going back at least as far as Ancient Greece where Homer used them in both *The Iliad* and *The Odyssey*. It is also believed that many English surnames were derived from nicknames around the 12th and 13th centuries. Not hard to imagine when you think of names like Longfellow, Whitehead, or Goodman.

Naturally, nicknames found their way into my writing and if you read my first novel, *Strip Cuts,* you will find them being used as one of the underlying themes. Through the writing, I found that I could express a lot about a character and how they were viewed in the community simply by giving them a nickname. Is it complimentary or derogatory? Does it have a profound meaning or no meaning at all? Does the character answer to it or not?

One of the other things I find intriguing is that when I ask where the name came from—especially in the case where someone has had a nickname for a couple of decades or more—often times, no one remembers. Another oddity of the nickname is why some of them stick while others fall away. If they do catch on, how long do they last? Sometimes, they drop off after a couple of months or when a person transitions, say, from high school to a college or into a career. In other cases, they are as permanent as a tattoo, staying with a person their whole life and even winding up in their obituary, between their first and last name: Jane "Kit-Kat" Smith.

Of course, this very thing has posed a bit of a problem for me since moving back to Clarion County. On a couple of occasions, I've run into an old acquaintance and wasn't sure if they still went by their nickname or not. On one hand, it felt a little weird calling them by their proper name when I never knew them that way. On the other hand, it was strange to hear myself saying, "How's it going, Pinhead?" to someone who was no longer a kid in my high school class, but now a construction worker, a high school principal, or a church pastor.

While nicknames can be used in a mean-spirited way, they are at their best when they are funny, lighthearted, or endearing. They connect people in an unusual and special way and offer an extra level of familiarity or friendliness.

Know what I mean, Bub?

WHAT NOW?

Last week, the air was crackling with the excitement of high school graduations. Fresh, young faces flush with the anticipation of total freedom and endless possibilities peered out from a sea of caps and gowns. Commencement speeches quoted great minds and cited examples of people who have led extraordinary lives, reminding those graduates to go after their dreams, to be kind and considerate, to trust their intuition, to be brave, and to live passionately. Emotions were high, and afterwards, parties and get-togethers were everywhere.

This week, however, I suspect some of those graduates are staring blankly at their diplomas—one of life's first major accomplishments—and thinking, "What now?"

While I would tell those newly-minted adults not to be afraid of that little question, I would also tell them to take it seriously and to get used to it because it will come up again and again for the rest of their lives. It will be there after their greatest successes and most humbling failures. It will show up at all of life's milestones and defining moments—good and bad—and it will be even more demanding during those periods where it feels like nothing at all is happening.

Seeing those caps tossed in the air last week and cars cruising up and down Main Street with the tassel dangling from the rearview mirror brought back long forgotten memories of my own high school graduation. This was inevitably followed by an assessment of where I thought I was heading back then, where I actually went, the things I managed to do right, what I wish I'd done differently, where I am at the present moment, and of course, that reoccurring question: What now?

It makes me miss that period of my life and wish I could go back and tell eighteen-year-old David what I know now. But who am I kidding? He wouldn't be able to comprehend it. He would listen and thank me because he was a polite kid, and he might even try to follow the advice, but he wouldn't get it. Like a lot of people, I've always accepted that life gets much harder as we get older, but now, as I remember 18, I have to admit that life was never easy. The problems are just different at each age. They seem easier when I look back because I've already faced those things, already figured them out, succeeded or failed, and either way, moved on from them.

That's not to say that life's been one long struggle either. Along with the difficulties of each age, there has also been lots of laughter, love, fun, rewards, and achievements. Which gets me to thinking of some of the commencement speeches I've heard over the years. I like the ones that are not too heavy-handed or sappy, and yet manage to be filled with hope and encouragement, quoting the likes of Goethe and Thoreau, daring the graduates to live each day as if their life has just begun, follow the beat of their own drum and move confidently in the direction of their dreams.

I wonder what it would be like if formal graduations continued throughout our adult lives. (I know this is impossible and I'm not suggesting such a thing in reality, but humor me for a few minutes.) What would it be like if we had a ceremony as we went from our 20s to our 30s, and every 10 years afterward for as long as we live? Each defining decade of our lives—the 40s, 50s, 60s, 70s, and beyond—would be noted and celebrated. Every 10 years, we'd don a cap and gown for an hour or two and look at where we are in our life, consider what happened over the past decade, reflect on how we've changed, ponder on our wins and losses, and then be treated to a commencement speech by some successful older person who had already passed through the decade we're heading into, and be offered advice and encouragement for meeting the challenges ahead. Then, we'd toss our caps in the air and party the night away.

And what about those commencement speeches?

The focus would be very different, of course, at 30 or 40, but would they be as positive and full of hope? Would they still encourage us to do our best, face life head on, celebrate the joy of being alive, and follow our dreams?

I would like to think so, because while life has never been easy, every decade I have been through (and I hope there are many more to come) has definitely been worth the price of admission.

So...what now?

I'd like to suggest that as we encourage those teenage graduates to make the most of their lives, we remember—regardless of what decade we are in—that the good advice we are offering applies to us as well.

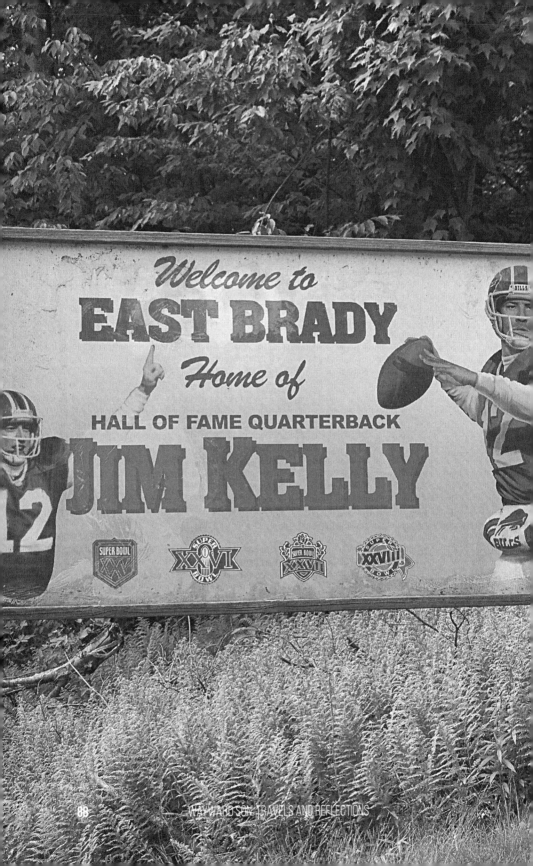

GRIDIRON GOLD

Last week, I had the privilege of attending Gridiron Gold at the Wyndham Grand Hotel in downtown Pittsburgh. The charity event successfully raised $800,000 dollars for the Neighborhood Legal Services Association, a non-profit organization that provides legal services to low-income individuals and families in southwestern Pennsylvania. The dinner, live auction, and panel discussion honored the six Pro Football Hall of Fame quarterbacks from western Pennsylvania. There are a total of 23 quarterbacks in the Hall of Fame at this time and a fourth of them were born and raised within a 60-mile radius of Pittsburgh. Along with East Brady's own Jim Kelly, there was Dan Marino (Pittsburgh), Joe Montana (New Eagle), George Blanda (Youngwood), Johnny Unitas (Pittsburgh), and Joe Namath (Beaver Falls).

Andrea Kremer, a chief correspondent for the NFL Network, led a roundtable discussion with the four surviving quarterbacks—Kelly, Marino, Montana, and Namath (the late Unitas and Blanda were represented by their families)—that was full of stories and a lot of laughs. The main question of the night, however, was one that has been asked by many football enthusiasts, commentators, and sportswriters over the years. That question was, "What is it about western Pennsylvania and great quarterbacks?"

Kelly said with a grin that it probably had something to do with all of them being conceived by parents drinking Iron City Beer. "Nah, seriously," he said, "those western Pennsylvania roots run deep. Our parents brought us up with a strong work ethic. My dad was a good example of that and taught me and my five brothers that if you want something, you have to work hard for it. Nothing is going to be handed to you on a silver platter."

Marino echoed the sentiment, saying that there was no doubt that the blue-collar mentality of not only working hard, but also treating people with respect, played a large part in his success. He mentioned the people he grew up with: "The games we played in the backyard were as important as the ones we played on the main stage. That's where you learned what was important."

All of the quarterbacks talked about how instrumental their fathers were in getting a ball in their hands early and encouraging them and driving them to be the best they could be. Growing up in a place that truly valued family, that taught the importance of it throughout life, was also central—a cornerstone of their success.

"Sports were a way out of a hard coalmining life," Montana said, "and taught good lessons. In that huddle, we were different races, religions, but with one purpose."

Namath, who all the others on the panel had watched and admired when they were growing up, said, "None of us got here on our own. It was the people we grew up with, the people who coached us." He cited the importance of the teammates around them as key players in their success, an opinion everyone on the panel cited repeatedly throughout the evening. "I followed all these guys through college," Namath said, nodding to Montana, Kelly, and Marino, "because they were from where I was from. Western PA! And I was a fan of all of them." While growing up, he watched Unitas and Blanda the same way the younger men had watched him.

"You can take the boys out of western Pennsylvania," Andrea Kremer said, bringing the evening to a close, "but you can't take western Pennsylvania out of the boys."

After hearing these Hall of Famers talk, I went back to the main question of the evening: What is it about western Pennsylvania and great quarterbacks? I think the question could be shortened: What is it about western Pennsylvania? Is there something special about this place? An enduring bond between the area and its people?

While my life has been vastly different from the ones these guys have led, I can absolutely relate to the things they noted as central to their upbringing: the blue-collar work ethic, being taught to treat people with respect, and knowing the importance of family. I know in my own life these things have fostered a certain resourcefulness, a never-say-die tenacity that somehow kept me going. I have to admit that growing up here, I spent most of my time concocting a plan to get out, see the world, and have adventures. I left Rimersburg in an old, rusted out Plymouth with enough money from bussing tables at Perkins and pumping gas at the Sligo General to survive a couple of weeks, maybe three if I skipped some meals.

Looking back, that was a plan fated for failure if there ever was one, but I somehow made it work. Whether I was harvesting corn in Iowa or acting professionally in Los Angeles, bartending in East Hampton or working as an Instructional Designer in Washington, DC, part of what the many people I met would often remember about me was where I was from. My accent (yes, we have one) gave me away as did my occasional use of words like "yinz" or "slippy," not to mention my unwavering loyalty to the Steelers.

The older I got, the more I embraced these pieces of western Pennsylvania that were, and always would be, a part of me. So, is there something special about western Pennsylvania?

You bet there is!

DODGING DOWNPOURS

Dodging downpours and riding between thunderstorms isn't ideal, but it beats waiting for inspiration and a stretch of good weather. I was patient all through May and now, with June three-quarters over, I'm done waiting. I'm on the road, taking my chances, winding through the lush Allegheny National Forest in northwestern Pennsylvania.

I grew up not far from here, but haven't traveled these roads in years and forgot about all of the logging trucks, tractor trailers, and tankers that travel these routes. They whip past, jolting the motorcycle and hitting me with a wave of hot, gritty air. As soon as possible, I switch to smaller roads, the kind with steep hills and tight turns that truckers tend to avoid.

I can't go through this part of the country without visiting Cook Forest. I was here several times as a boy and revisiting it now is like rereading a great book. It's even better with time, comfortably familiar and yet, somehow, new again.

Continuing north, I also stop off at the Kinzua Bridge. It is a testament to both man's ingenuity and nature's final word. When it was built in 1882, it was the tallest railroad bridge in the world. At 301 feet, it was higher than the Brooklyn Bridge. Even more amazing, they rebuilt it in 1900, concurrently taking it apart and putting it back together, replacing the iron with steel so it could handle more weight. The new six-and-a-half-million-pound structure was operational for over a hundred years. Then, a tornado whipped through in 2003 and in a matter of seconds, did this:

The cost of rebuilding wouldn't be a profitable venture in today's world so it's been turned into a visitor's park. Part of the structure still stands and has been rebuilt to include a glass skywalk. My pictures don't do it justice; it's worth seeing in person.

Speaking of the power of nature, after zigzagging another couple of hours eastward, I come across the remains of the Austin Dam in Potter County. After splashing through a rough, muddy road, I reach a memorial park with pictures from before and after the dam's collapse.

KINZUA BRIDGE

There is also literature telling its history, including how it failed on September 30, 1911, wiping out the town of Austin and drowning 78 people.

One of the stories I read is about a woman named Cora Brooks, who was a bit of an outcast in Austin because she ran a brothel. Her home was on a hill nearby and she was one of the very first to see the dam break. She called the switchboard operators in town urging them to sound the alarms and tell everyone to run to higher ground immediately. Her message got through and she is credited with saving hundreds of lives.

With the wind picking up and the sky turning black, it doesn't look like I am going to be going anywhere for a while so I pull the bike under a pavilion and get comfortable on top of a picnic table. A few minutes later, the sky opens up and rain pounds the roof of the pavilion.

I take the notepad out of my back pocket and give myself a reminder to do some research on Cora Brooks when I get home. I also jot down other thoughts and images of the day, looking for something I can spin into a future short story, a column, or an article.

Looking at the ruined dam in the pouring rain, it's not hard to imagine what happened here on the last day of September in 1911.

AUSTIN DAM IN POTTER COUNTY, PA

GHOSTS

It is strange how these trips often take on a certain motif without me directing it. Yesterday, for example, it was impossible not to be aware of the dictating forces of nature as I was "Dodging Downpours" and witnessing examples of the power of nature, whether it was how a tornado brought down the great Kinzua Bridge or how a wall of water pushed aside a concrete dam and wiped out a town.

Today, the theme seems to be...ghosts.

It started when I arrived in Coudersport. I'd once read of a hotel where Eliot Ness was said to have written The Untouchables. How he got from the mean streets of Chicago during the Prohibition era to this quaint, little town in north, central Pennsylvania a couple decades later, I had no clue, but I figured if the place was still in business, I'd grab a beer and a bite to eat there. I parked on the Main Street and was stopped by this amazing looking place:

If ever a house looked like it should be haunted, this would be it. I found out it has been long abandoned and unless someone with the means to restore it comes along pretty soon, its days are numbered, which would be a shame. Built in the late 1870s as the dream home of a wealthy businessman, it has had many incarnations since. And yes, there is a ghost story. In 1928, it became the Old Hickory Tavern and—according to local lore—a young man was shot there in a barroom brawl and carried upstairs where he later died. Over the many decades since, people claim to have seen a young man standing at the upstairs window gazing out into the night.

Also on Main Street, I found the Hotel Crittenden and lunch. Eliot Ness did indeed move to Coudersport and supposedly did like to drink at the bar and tell stories of his glory days as a Prohibition

COUDERSPORT, PA

agent in Chicago. With a lot of help from a sports writer named Oscar Fraley, he did write much of his memoir at a corner table in what is now the restaurant.

I tried to get a room for the night there but they were renovating the hotel part of the building, so I was back on the road where I encountered an even bigger ghost story a few towns away in Smethport.

I stopped off at the Old Jail Museum where, for five bucks, I got a guided tour of the oldest public building in town. Built in 1872 and used as a jail until 1990, the place is packed with local history, original artifacts from the Civil War, and memorabilia of the area's lumber, oil, and railroad past. For anyone interested in history, this visit is well worth the time.

But back to the ghost story...

It is well documented that 11 men were hanged on the third floor of the jail. The most famous was a man by the name of Ralph Crossmire, who was hanged for the murder of his mother in 1893. Crossmire swore he was innocent to the very end, and as they led him to his death, he swore if they carried out the hanging, he would return and haunt the jail. Within days after his death—and countless times over the years since—inmates and guards claimed to have seen Crossmire's ghost. Even today, visitors and workers at the museum have made similar claims.

THE CRIME AVENGED !

Ralph Crossmire Hanged by the Neck until Dead

IN THE CORRIDOR OF OUR COUNTY JAIL !

Jerked into Eternity by a Two Hundred and Forty Pound Weight Falling Four Feet in Mid Air.

While the 3rd floor is not yet open to the public, the dungeon is. Massive stones make up eight cold, damp, dark rooms where a prisoner was confined as a form of punishment. My tour guide stayed in the doorway as I wandered through the area. "I don't even like to think of what it must have been like when they locked the door," she said, "and shut off the lights."

By the time I left the museum, another storm was moving in. Dark clouds filled the rearview mirror, but there was a patch of blue sky off in the distance in the direction I was headed. I focused on that and made a run for it.

OLD JAIL MUSEUM, COUDERSPORT, PA

HAPPY TRAILS

I took my first real motorcycle trip of the year last week, traveling through north-central Pennsylvania on a two-day ride. Dodging downpours and getting stranded a time or two, I realized that even the difficulties added to the trip. They put a little drama in the story and forced me to think on my feet. That got me thinking about road trips in general and how they are good for the soul.

If you've never taken a random road trip—or if it's been a long time since you have—I highly recommend doing so. Though I am partial to a motorcycle, any vehicle will work. You don't need a lot of money or time (an overnight trip is fine). Take your family or a couple of close friends or make it a romantic get-away with your spouse. If coordinating schedules is a hassle, you can always take off on your own. In fact, I think everyone should do a solo trip at least once in their life just to experience the freedom of an itinerary that is determined entirely by you.

Road trips are a miracle cure for monotony. It allows you to unplug from the daily grind and with the wind blowing through your hair and a great song on the radio, you're free. No schedule to keep, no to-do list to worry about. There is nothing like the open road to remind you of all the possibilities in life and awaken your sense of wonder. You can't help but reconnect with yourself and the landscape and whoever is traveling with you.

As for finding a place to go, get creative. Choose a place a few hours away that you've always been meaning to go but have just never found the time. Or get on the Internet and look up "things to do" in a city or a national park within driving distance. Or my personal favorite: Just start driving and go wherever the road takes you.

There is no need to do much planning as part of the fun is letting the day unfold. I do, however, suggest getting an early start and having a good breakfast so you won't be hungry for a while. I also throw together a light lunch—a sandwich, a piece of fruit, a bottle of water—just enough to sustain you but not really fill you up.

Even if you have a specific destination, stay open to being drawn off course if something pulls at you. The uncertainty that freaks us out in everyday life can be embraced here. By late afternoon, you'll have worked up a good appetite and can start looking for the perfect place to spend it. Avoid fast food or something you can throw together at home. Find an interesting place to land and ask around to see where the locals eat. It will probably be delicious, reasonably priced, and it will also tell you something about that town and the people who live there.

This brings up another important point: talk to strangers. Ask questions. I am quiet by nature, but I push myself to be more extroverted on these outings. Eating at the bar also makes talking to people easier. Along with the bartender, you have whoever is sitting to your left and your right. Not everyone is friendly, but most people are and it is usually well worth the effort. You will be surprised how little some people know about the place they have lived their whole lives, but you will also meet incredibly knowledgeable people who are so thrilled that an outsider cares about their little town, that they will tell you anything and everything you could possibly want to know about local attractions and things to do in the area.

Finally, don't go with great expectations. Let it be whatever it is. The real purpose of these excursions is to relax and reconnect with who you are and where you're at in your life. You may very well end up with a great story to tell or a new insight, which is great. But even if you don't, you will have, at the very least, broken your routine, visited a new place, and met some new people.

So ... happy trails!

SLEEP FIGHTER

Even though it is still dark outside, the morning birds are already chirping, singing their songs, heralding a new day. Normally, I would welcome these cheerful and peaceful sounds, but this morning, they echo through the pre-dawn darkness like a message saying, "Sorry, bud, time's up! You missed your chance." For the past 3 days, I have been wrestling with sleeplessness and according to those birds, I just lost another match: Insomnia 3 – David 0.

So...this column is going to be a little different than my usual fare. Having slept about 5 tattered hours in the past 72, the majority of my focus is fixated on two questions. One, what do I have to do to get some sleep? And two, the most immediate and pressing, where in the next 8 to 10 hours can I sneak in a nap?

Yes, I know that conventional wisdom says naps are the bad guys; they are counterproductive. They offer a few minutes of sleep and a refreshing battery recharge, but then turn around and make it even harder to sleep at night, aiding and abetting insomnia, which is the enemy. I am not so sure this is true. In the past, when I've tried fighting the allure of naps in hopes of cashing in on that promised full night of sleep, it never worked out for me. More often than not, after dragging all day, when bedtime finally arrived, instead of getting sleepy, I got a second wind. What's weird is that even under normal circumstances, I find getting 8 solid hours of sleep impossible and yet, I can dive into a nap as easily as Antonio Brown transitions from a touchdown reception to a victory dance.

Unfortunately, these bouts of insomnia are not new territory, happening at least once a year for as long as I can remember. According to my mom, from infancy right on through childhood, I was a "sleep-fighter."

"It's like you were afraid you were going to miss something if you went to sleep," she said. And I do remember feeling exactly like that. As soon as I was sure Mom and Dad were asleep, I'd sneak downstairs and watch TV or move stealthily through the house with a flashlight, pretending I was looking for a treasure or clues to some great mystery until the lights came on and an exhausted-looking parent marched me back to bed. But, as a kid, it was cool. It felt like I had a superpower because I didn't need to sleep like regular kids. This was not true, of course, and by the time I was an adult who had to get up and go to work in the morning, I knew full well that being awake most of the night was not cool, super, or powerful.

However, I'd already developed some very bad habits when it came to sleeping. "You never learned to sleep," one doctor told me, which made me feel like I was flunking a class no one else even had to take.

As the sun comes up and spills through the room, I see the pamphlet titled "How to Conquer Insomnia" that I'd read from cover to cover last night. According to its pages, I'm not alone. About 60 million Americans are affected by sleep disorders. The pamphlet is one of the many my mom has given me over the years in her tireless effort to help me find a lasting solution. Along with pamphlets like this, she has given me articles she'd cut out of magazines, books she'd bought containing the secrets of sleep, and CDs she'd ordered with meditations and soothing sounds guaranteed to ease me into a nurturing slumber. Some of the advice and meditative sounds worked temporarily, but nothing has really solved the problem for good. Mostly, the literature gave the same advice, telling me to cut out coffee, pop, beer, and evening snacks while keeping to a routine, going to bed early and at the same time each night. (While this nearly bored me to death, it never really helped me sleep.)

As I get ready, I come back to that burning question about where I am going to grab that nap. Finding a place in the middle of a workday—even on a lunch break—isn't all that easy. Unless you are in kindergarten, our society tends to frown on naps. I visited Spain a few years back and noticed that every day around mid-afternoon, the streets went quiet. "Where is everyone?" I asked. "Siesta," was the answer I received.

That's right. Everyone was taking a nap, like they do every afternoon.

What a great idea! If there really are 60 million others like me out there, maybe I could start a trend.

WAYWARD SON: TRAVELS AND REFLECTIONS

TO WHAT END?

When I was just starting out as a writer, I was asked a question that took me off guard, confused me at the time, and kept returning years afterward. I'd fallen in love with a girl during my last year at the University of Pittsburgh and was meeting her family for the first time. At that point, I'd lived most of my life in Rimersburg; she was from East Hampton, New York. It didn't matter to either of us that we'd grown up in two totally different worlds. In fact, it made the relationship all the more romantic. I do, however, have to admit to feeling more than a little conspicuous driving into her hometown in an old Ford Escort with a bad paint job, winding through the mansion-lined streets that celebrities like Martha Stewart, Calvin Klein, and Billy Joel called home.

Things started off very well though. I was a hit with her mother and her sisters. During dinner, they wanted to know all about my writing, what I was working on, where I got my ideas, and who my favorite authors were. It was going so well, I'd almost forgotten about her father, an engineer and self-made millionaire who was far from convinced that I was worthy of dating his beautiful daughter. (A rookie mistake on my part, I know, but what can I say? I was a rookie!) While I waxed philosophical about my dream of writing novels, he unceremoniously broke into the conversation with the question, "To what end?"

The table went quiet. I wasn't sure I understood the question but did my best to answer and talked about my passion for writing. He stopped me by holding up a hand, and in so many words, said that he wasn't interested in my passions or my dreams. He wanted to know why I thought writing stories for a living—a vocation that not only seemed silly to him, but practically guaranteed poverty—was a worthwhile thing to do with my life.

I'd like to say I silenced him with a suave, witty answer, but blindsided by the question, in unfamiliar territory (I was still trying to figure out why each place at the table had three different sized forks), I couldn't come up with anything remotely suave or witty.

I held my ground though, looked him in the eye, and defended my direction in life and the passion behind it. This earned me further favor with the ladies at the table and put him in the doghouse for being rude to the dinner guest. At any rate, the awkward moment passed and we went on to have a pleasant evening.

Still, that question—"To what end?"—stuck with me, and I made myself answer it more fully, not for him, but for myself. I answered it then and I have come back to answer it again and again throughout the years.

I could do a whole column on how human beings—across all cultures—have been using stories to make sense of our lives, to record history, educate and entertain from the first cave drawings to the latest bestselling books and blockbuster films. Heck, I could write a whole book on it. And then another one on why it is so important to me, despite the difficulties of trying to scratch out a living doing it. But the short answer is that I write stories to connect, to encourage people to laugh, to get a little teary-eyed, to think, and to inspire them to share their own stories, not necessarily in writing, but verbally with others.

Asking "to what end" has focused me when I am adrift, in part, because it inspires a lot of other questions. What am I doing? Why am I doing it? Why do I care? And the all-important and ever-changing question: What do I want?

Regardless of what stage of life you are in, whether you are raising a family, building or maintaining a business, planning for retirement, or just trying to keep things afloat, I think this is a valuable question to ask yourself. It is surprisingly hard to answer, especially if you are feeling a little uninspired or uncertain. But if you make the effort to answer it as fully as you can, you will find that it can ground you and reconnect you with where you are, where you're going, and whether you still want to go there or not.

So, look at what you are doing with the precious remaining hours of your life and ask yourself, "To what end?"

By the way, the man who first asked me that question has since passed away and despite our rocky introduction, we went on to be pretty good buddies. His daughter and I were together for quite a while and when we decided not to get married after all and went our separate ways, he admitted that he was a little sad about that.

What changed his mind about me? The stories I wrote. *Strip Cuts* turned out to be one of his all-time favorite books. He read it several times.

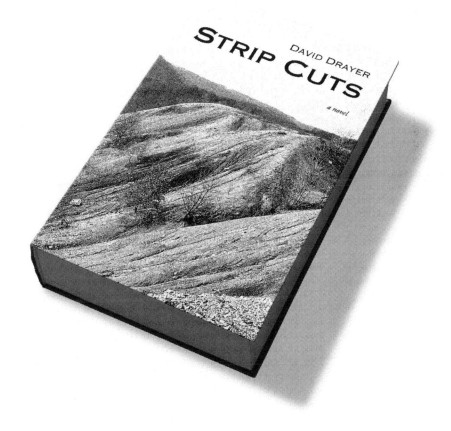

Dave Drayer

Dave Drayer

Sort of HOLLYWOOD ACTOR

Rummaging through a bin of five-dollar movies at the Walmart in Clarion, a friend held up a copy of *As Good as It Gets*, the Oscar-winning film starring Jack Nicholson, and said, "Weren't you in this movie?"

"Sort of," I said, "but not really." I was also sort-of-but-not-really in *The Last Samurai*, *The Adventures of Rocky and Bullwinkle*, and some episodes of *Melrose Place*. I'd worked as an "extra" in these shows. (The term has since been changed to the more politically correct "background actor.") In other words, I was hired to be in the background, to help create atmosphere while not stealing focus from the scene that was being shot. While I was a somewhat accomplished actor on the stage when I arrived in Los Angeles in the late 90s, I had no money, no agent, and not a single contact in the movie business. I figured extra work would be my way through the impenetrable gates of Hollywood, and I was—sort of, but not really—correct.

I went to cattle call auditions, which were open to anyone, and sent my picture to agencies that specialized in background actors. Almost immediately, I was being told to report to the Paramount Lot or Universal Studios. I was ecstatic! I will never forget walking onto a studio lot with an old western town complete with a dusty street and an old saloon on my right, while to my left, there was a New York subway station, its walls covered with Broadway posters and graffiti. I could hardly believe I was working on the same sets as actors like Tom Cruise and Robert De Niro. I saw Jennifer Aniston leaving the lot one day and instinctually waved at her. She smiled and waved back. How bizarre.

Most of the background actors I worked with were doing the same thing I was: trying to get in the door as an actor, to get that essential big break, to get seen. And yet, we were all hired to be unnoticed and unseen. I was fascinated by this peculiar contradiction and started taking note of what I was seeing around me. After a while, I realized that most productions were basically looking for two types of people depending on the kind of show it was: PPs (pretty people) or very unusual looking people. Pretty people were a dime a dozen in LA, so it was the unusual-looking ones that I'd catch silently critiquing each other's "look," pouting if someone else looked too much like them, and envious of characteristics that would never normally be coveted, like a weirdly-shaped head, bug eyes, or huge ears.

It was a very strange experience. One guy I worked with claimed to be the Ugly Naked Guy on *Friends* (the hottest show on television at that time). Who knows if he was telling the truth because part of the show's gimmick was that you never actually saw the Ugly Naked Guy. Only in Hollywood would someone brag about being the Ugly Naked Guy, and not only would he brag about it, but he would use it as a pick-up line with the multitude of pretty, young actresses gathered in the holding room where all the extras waited to be called on set.

And it worked! I saw the alleged Ugly Naked Guy approach woman after woman and after chatting them up for a few minutes, walk away with a phone number. I overheard him saying things like, "I'll talk to my agent and see what I can do," or "Let's do lunch and I'll give you some pointers."

I never realized how hard being an extra would be on my soul. I'd been in over 20 professional plays at that point, often in lead roles, and there I was playing Guy Waiting for Bus, or while partnered with an actress, Attractive Couple Having Lunch. I did one scene where they filmed me and another guy from the knees down. They needed a shot of shoes walking across a grating. The other actor kept asking me who our characters were and what our motivation was. "Dude," I said, "they are filming our feet. They just want us to walk 10 feet and walk back."

"But what's our motivation?"

"To get to the other side and pick up our paychecks."

"You best get a better attitude, mister," he said to me, "or you're never going to make it in this town."

I guess he was right. I gave up extra work shortly after that, realizing that once casting directors recognized you as a background actor, they'd never consider you for a speaking part. I stayed in LA for seven years though, and did have a measure of success playing the lead in an independent film and getting bit parts here and there, but so much of the time spent was about networking and constantly selling myself. I was not very good at, or interested in, doing either. Though I still love acting, my personality is much more suited to writing.

I never watched *Melrose Place* or *The Last Samurai*, so I don't know if I appear on screen or not. *As Good as It Gets* was such a good movie that I forgot to look for myself in the background. However, 21 minutes into *The Adventures of Rocky and Bullwinkle*, I can be spotted —sort of, but not really— doing a scene with Robert De Niro, Rene Russo, and Jason Alexander.

INTO THE STORM

It's mid-morning and I'm on the motorcycle heading east through Cook Forest in northwestern Pennsylvania. The air is alive with one of my favorite summer smells, a combination of sunbaked pine trees, the river, and wood smoke lingering from last night's campfires. I just finished the first draft of a novella and hopped on the bike both to celebrate and to forget about the story for a while. Between doing research, getting to know the characters, and writing the narrative, it has consumed my thoughts for the past...I don't know how many weeks...and I need to let go of it for a bit, think about other things, other stories I want to write.

Already, the day is hot and I appreciate the sections of the road where the trees keep pockets of air so cold that they cause a prickle of chills to shoot up my arms and down my back. The saddlebags are packed for a trip of two or three days, but I can stretch it out longer if I want. As usual, I have no specific destination in mind. I pass a bar in Sigel that looks vaguely familiar. Then, I remember dancing there a couple of years ago with an ex-girlfriend from DC. My sister and brother-in-law had taken us there on a visit to western PA. We had a blast. I remember the four of us dancing until they started shutting off the lights.

I am near Clear Creek and am reminded of a spot I wanted to visit in this area called Beartown Rocks. An acquaintance who reads my blog and column had recommended it. I stop at a ranger station for directions and find I am only a few miles away. It is supposedly a jumble of rocks as big as houses created by the glacier. I park the motorcycle and spend the next while walking through them. They are amazing!

BEARTOWN ROCKS, CLEAR CREEK STATE FOREST, PA

I continue east, avoiding highways, zigzagging my way through forests and small towns. Even though my saddlebags are too full to carry anything else, I can't resist stopping at a roadside stand selling homegrown vegetables. They have cucumbers, tomatoes, corn, zucchini, and peppers. I buy a handful of cherry tomatoes and an ice-cold bottle of water and take them to a shady spot where I can consult the map and see where I am.

The tomatoes taste like summer, slightly tangy, almost sweet. I dig out the map and find that I am a couple hours away from another place I have heard about. Ricketts Glen State Park is in Luzerne County and is supposed to have 24 named waterfalls ranging in size from 9 to 94 feet.

So, I guess that's where I'm heading next.

I arrive at Ricketts Glen around 4:00 in the afternoon. The sky has turned dark and an ominous wind is kicking up. I have been on the bike for about six hours zigzagging my way across the state. My plan of spending the last few hours of the day hiking is in danger of being rained out.

I am going to need a room for the night so I suppose I could skip the hike and go in search of a motel, but my phone has no signal here and something tells me there is nothing close by. Besides, getting back on the road under that sky would be crazier than setting out on a hike. Taking shelter under the pavilion at the edge of the parking lot is the wisest move.

I stretch out muscles cramped from the hours on the bike and intend to wait out the storm, but the trail looks so inviting that I

RICKETTS GLEN STATE PARK, PA

can't resist starting down the path, telling myself I won't go far. The forest is deep and dark and has an energy that I want to absorb. Or maybe it is absorbing me as I keep getting pulled in, further and further. I pass a family of five rushing in the opposite direction. "There's a storm blowing in," the father says to me. "You're going to want to turn around and get back to the parking lot."

While that is probably what I should do, it is the last thing I *want* to do. So, I keep going...

Every time I am about to turn around, I come to another stunning waterfall or a picture I can't resist walking into. This is one of the most beautiful parks I have ever been to and I am absolutely high on the splendor of it.

A tremendous crack of thunder echoes through the dark woods. I hear the rain hitting the leaves overhead before I feel it and then it is hissing all around me, drenching me along with everything else. Getting wet isn't the bad part though. The bad part is that the rocks that line the often steep slopes were once in the creek bed and, in the rain, they become very slippery.

I find a huge overhanging rock and take shelter there. Watching the storm, I fish out the notebook that I always carry in my back pocket and write down notes from the day.

Occasionally, a small group of hikers braving the rain come by, slipping and sliding, scaling up the trail, their clothes hanging heavy and wet, and their hair plastered to their heads. For the most part, they seem to take it in stride, accepting it as part of the experience. Most don't notice me sitting cross-legged under the over-hang, out of the rain, writing in my notebook. The ones that do sort of startle and then pretend they saw me all along. I usually wave and they mostly wave back. One girl, college-aged, shouts, "Are you drawing in that book?"

"Writing," I shout back.

She smiles and nods. "Perfect place to do it."

After about a half-hour, the rain stops and I continue on the trail, seeing one waterfall after the other. The late afternoon sun returns then making everything shimmer as I make it back to my bike.

RICKETTS GLEN STATE PARK, PA

GETTING LUCKY

Is it better to be talented or lucky? Which would you rather be?

An old friend and I were discussing this on the phone the other night. It is a question she and I have revisited many times throughout our long friendship. The conversation started over 20 years ago when we were working in East Hampton, New York. We were a couple back then and were saving money to move to Los Angeles and take our shot at the big time.

During that summer, I worked as a landscaper and she worked as a house cleaner. In the evenings, we both worked for her mother's catering business, serving food, washing dishes, tending bar, and anything else that needed to be done. When her mother got a call for someone to wash dishes and serve wine for a small dinner party at the home of Joseph Heller—the writer who coined the phrase "Catch-22" in his world-famous novel by the same name—she gave me the job.

Along with Mr. and Mrs. Heller, there were two other couples in attendance. I poured the wine and cleared the plates, but mostly, I was in the kitchen keeping the dishes washed. At one point, one of the guests came in the kitchen to see what wine was being served and introduced himself as Marshall Brickman. I recognized the name as that of a screenwriter. We started to talk and I told him I was a writer, too—though at the time, I was years away from publishing anything—and asked if he had any advice. Talent and hard work were a given, he said, but the real secret of success was luck.

This was disappointing. I could keep honing whatever talent I had and I could continue to work hard, but how was I supposed to get lucky?

He offered his story to back-up his belief, telling me that many years ago he saw this unknown comedian performing at a comedy club that he frequented in the city. "I thought he was hilarious. I'd go talk to him when he came off stage and we became friends. He said he wanted to write a screenplay and asked me if I'd collaborate with him. I said sure, why not? Well, that guy turned out to be Woody Allen." It was a turning point in Brinkman's career. He wrote three screenplays with Allen, including *Annie Hall*, which won him an Oscar in 1978, and went on to write many other pieces on his own for the stage and screen.

The other gentleman came in the kitchen then and Marshall introduced us and posed the question to him. I no longer recall the man's name, but I remember he was a very wealthy and successful businessman who owned a company that manufactured titanium. "Luck," he said, without hesitation.

"You guys are killing me."

He shrugged and told me his story then. When he was in high school, he had a crush on a girl and asked her out. Her father was extremely old-fashioned and did not allow her to date unless he met and approved of the boy first. "I got to know the family and the old man gave his permission," he said. "Well, the girl and I went out for a bit, but things didn't work out between us. However, I really hit it off with her father. He had a very successful business in titanium. He gave me a job and taught me everything he knew about the business, and by the time he was ready to retire, I was in a position to take over."

All three of the women came in then, looking for the missing dinner guests. Marshall filled them in and posed the question to them: Is it better to be talented or lucky? His wife, a television producer, was about to answer when Joseph Heller came in the kitchen and saw us all huddled around the sink, me with a hand towel draped over my shoulder. He put his hands on his hips and said, in a thick Brooklyn accent, "David. May I have my party back?"

"Oh. Sure."

He looked at his wife and said, "I told ya not to hire a writer."

"Who said he was a writer?" she asked.

"Are ya kidding? I can tell to look at him."

I took this as a compliment, although, looking back, I'm not so sure he meant it as one. As they were returning to the living room, his wife asked him what he thought was more important, talent or luck. "Luck," he said, "of course."

At the end of the night, I met my then-girlfriend at the beach—part of our routine that summer—where we swapped stories about our day and evening jobs. Despite hearing from three very successful people, neither of us believed it was luck back then. We couldn't afford to believe that. Our dreams were too far off. We didn't dare throw up our hands and just hope to get lucky.

My answer has changed continuously over the years, and to be honest with you, I really don't know how I would answer that question today. So, I ask you: Would you rather be talented or lucky?

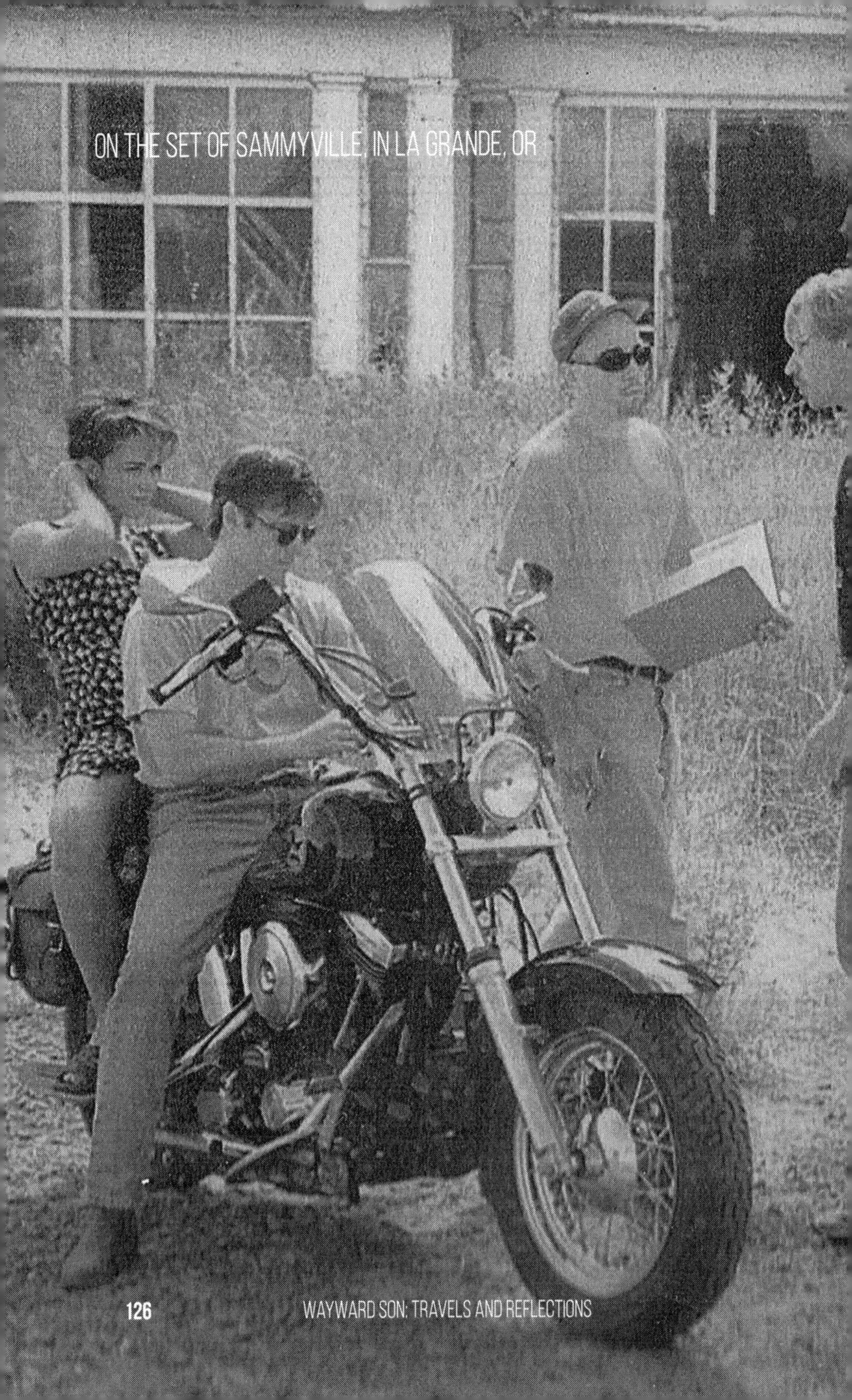

ON THE SET OF SAMMYVILLE, IN LA GRANDE, OR

FOOTBALL PHILOSOPHY

Ah, yes, the national football season is upon us: fierce rivalries, trash talk, roaring crowds, world-class athletes giving their all for a moment in the spotlight, hitting hard, soaring through the air, breaking records by willing the human body to do amazing things while cheerleaders dance, commentators analyze, and fans—in stadiums and living rooms across the country—don the jerseys of their favorite players and go mad with football fever.

It's great to be in western Pennsylvania this season, rooting for the black and gold in Steeler country, enjoying the games with my family. I usually try to catch another NFL game or two over the weekend as well. I love the physicality and competitiveness of football, but over time, the game has taken on a much deeper meaning for me. What I see happening on the field is more than just a game: it's a microcosm of life itself. I can get downright philosophical about it and I probably drive people crazy by speaking in football metaphors from September to February. When I was teaching, I told my composition students as we neared the end of the semester that I expected them to "play the full 60 minutes" and warned them about the dangers of "dropping the ball in the fourth quarter."

I remember a lot of blank stares.

The first time I saw football in this larger sense was when I was filming on location in Oregon some years ago. I was working on an independent movie that I'd co-written and was playing the lead in, called *Sammyville* (AKA *Dark Woods*). We were on a shoestring budget, everything was on the line, and anything that could have possibly gone wrong, was going wrong. Everyone in the cast and crew was getting the flu, one person had a nervous breakdown, several others were fighting, some were quitting, others getting fired, we were having technical difficulties and running out of time and money to finish the film. On our only day off, exhausted and trying not to get depressed, I went to a local bar to lose myself in a football game. There was only one TV screen in the small-town tavern and it was playing a Kansas City-Seattle game.

The game was being played through a heavy downpour. The water and mud were inches deep on the field and the rain was coming down so hard I could barely make out who were the Chiefs and who were the Seahawks. (I later found out that five inches of rain fell on the area and caused flash flooding throughout Kansas City. The game would be dubbed "The Mud Bowl.")

I was mesmerized. Despite not being able to get any kind of footing, see more than a few feet in front of them, and having great difficulty holding on to the ball, both teams were not just playing, but playing hard, playing to win. They were resourceful in finding ways to move the ball in conditions that were practically impossible. In spite of the circumstances, they were playing down and dirty, smash-mouth football and no one was about to give up without a fight. It rejuvenated me, fired me up at a time when I really needed it and inspired me to find the strength to keep on giving my all to the film regardless of the deteriorating conditions.

I became aware of the teamwork too, which is one of the things that was sorely lacking in our production. I noticed how each player was dependent on the others. One person couldn't win a football game. Not even a superstar. A great quarterback, for example, is powerless without the protection of the line and the receivers who can get open and catch the ball.

Since then, I have viewed football differently and am continually amazed at the life lessons and motivation that can be gleaned just from watching the game. Discipline, focus, persistence, the importance of preparation, and consistency are a must for any successful team.

I am also amazed that despite the criticism the NFL has come under in the last few years—most of it deserved—the love of the game still manages to bring millions of people together across generational, religious, racial, geographic, and political divides.

So, if you see me watching hour after hour of football this weekend, remember, I am not simply wasting time. I am studying philosophy.

That's my story and I'm sticking to it.

HOLDING ON AND LETTING GO

It is a bright, sunny morning and I am riding my motorcycle north through the Allegheny National Forest, packed for what I am guessing will be a 2 to 3-day excursion. The fog is just starting to lift from the river and the scenic route between Tionesta and Tidioute is heavily shaded by hills and trees. It is a beautiful scene but so sheltered from the sun that the air is frigid, and I am kicking myself for not putting leather chaps over my jeans and a sweatshirt under my jacket. Of course, this is always part of a motorcycle trip in the fall. With cold mornings, hot afternoons, and the very limited space of two small saddlebags, packing is always difficult, presenting the same dilemma: what can I leave behind and what is necessary to have with me?

That's an interesting idea to consider in a figurative sense as well. What can we let go of and leave behind in life? What do we need to hold onto and carry with us?

To keep my mind off of the fact that I am freezing, I ponder those questions and by the time I am approaching the New York state line, I am listing off some answers. Regret, I have to say, would be a good thing to get rid of. And bad habits. Guilt, too, isn't much good once you realize you've screwed up. Anger. Grudges.

Most people would probably agree that those are good things to let go of, and yet, most of us have a hard time doing it. For example, if you've ever been betrayed or hurt by someone—and who hasn't?—you feel you have every right to be angry. And you most certainly do. But it doesn't change the fact that sooner or later, you need to unpack it and leave it behind because it is heavy, it takes up a lot of room, and it is pretty much useless on the trip.

Thinking turns out to be a good distraction. The temperature continues to rise and I am no longer cold by the time I am cruising through farmland in upstate New York. I randomly take whatever road looks interesting to me and find myself leisurely zigzagging between Cattaraugus and Chautauqua counties amid apple and grape orchards. It is an excellent day for motorcycling and now I'm glad that I didn't wear the chaps and sweatshirt because it would be too hot now and there's no room for them in the saddlebags anyway.

As the day winds down, I start looking for a place to spend the night and come to a bright blue Victorian house with a white picket fence and a vacancy sign in the window. It overlooks a lake and I have to stop and check it out. I am greeted on the sun porch by a woman in her mid-fifties with long hair wearing a tie-dyed dress and no shoes or socks. Since it is the off-season and they don't get many tourists in October, she quotes me a very reasonable price for the night and I accept. Before escorting me to my room, she asks me to remove my shoes and leave them on the porch. We ascend a narrow, creaky staircase to the second floor where there are three bedrooms. Every room has two twin beds draped with colorful, old-fashioned quilts and is nicely decorated with antique dressers and nightstands. She tells me the house was built in 1886 and I make a joke about old houses being haunted. "There are spirits that live here, yes," she says nonchalantly, "and you very well might hear them throughout the night, but I wouldn't call the place haunted."

Yikes!

She hands me fresh towels and points to the single bathroom shared by all the guests. "But you will have it all to yourself," she says, "because you are the only guest tonight."

Double yikes!

I unpack, shower off the road, and find a bar within walking distance. I have a steak sandwich and fries for dinner while making small talk with the bartender and a couple of locals. On the walk back, I notice that the night has gotten cool. A hint of wood smoke from a nearby fireplace mixes with the smell of the lake and the crisp, fall air. I stop in front of the place before going inside and take it all in: the old, blue house, the picket fence, my motorcycle the only vehicle in the small parking lot, my room the only light on the second floor. I couldn't possibly have imagined when I set out on the motorcycle this morning that I'd be spending the night as the only guest (not counting "the spirits," of course) in an old Victorian house in upstate New York.

My mind revisits the question that I started off the day with, realizing that I never got around to answering the second part of it, the part about the things I do want to carry with me. The only thing I can think of at the moment is this sense of adventure, this sense of wonder, and how I hope I always carry that with me. For who knows what tomorrow might bring, who I might meet, and what I might experience so long as I stay open to wherever the road might lead.

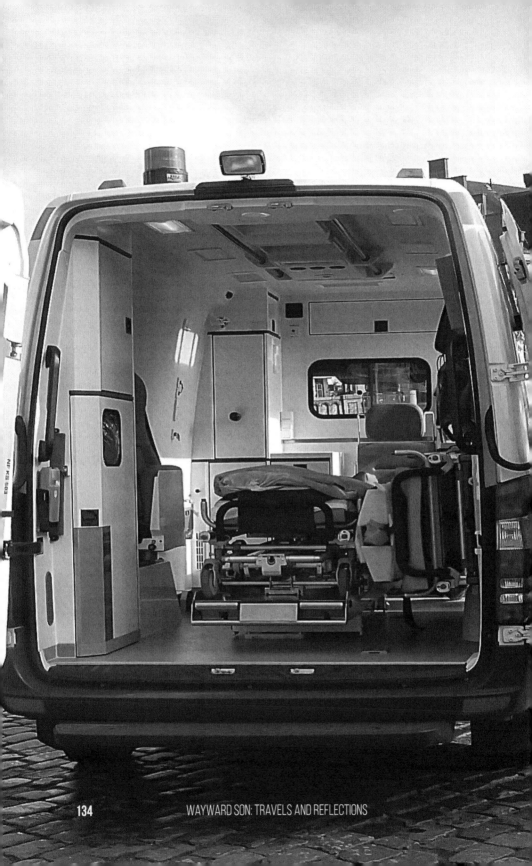

AMBULANCE WORKERS

Recently, I was writing a short story where one of the characters worked on an ambulance crew. Knowing nothing about the life of ambulance workers—for starters, they don't like being called "ambulance workers"—I knew I needed to do some research before I could continue writing. Fortunately, my sister, Susan, is the secretary for the Southern Clarion County Ambulance Service (SCCAS) located between Rimersburg and Sligo. "Do you think some of the people you work with would let me interview them?" I asked.

"They might," she said, "if you bring them doughnuts."

Fair enough.

I met with two separate crews of emergency medical technicians (EMTs) and paramedics. I explained that I needed to know what their day to day life was like and started by asking why they chose this line of work.

"This is going to be a short interview," Troy, a paramedic with over 20 years of experience working both here and in Clarion said. "I can answer that in three words: We are crazy."

Everyone nodded in agreement, that yeah, they were nuts. Fred, a paramedic and the Director of Operations elaborated. "Think about it. We work long hours and all shifts, including holidays and weekends. The job is stressful, the responsibility is high, and the pay is low."

"Okay," I said, "but aside from being crackers, why do you do it?"

Matt, an EMT and recent addition to the crew, cited the challenge of thinking on your feet and "always being on." Others mentioned the adrenaline rush and the variety of every day being different, but the most popular answer and the one everyone agreed with, was the idea of helping people, making a difference, having the opportunity to save a life. "Sometimes," Ethan, an EMT, added, "a person will need a hand to hold or a shoulder to cry on, and a lot of times, we are that hand or that shoulder."

"It sounds corny," Amy, a paramedic, shrugged, "but it's true."

"Another thing about the job," Ethan said, "is the camaraderie."

Troy looked at him. "That's a pretty big word for you, isn't it?"

"It is," Ethan agreed, "and it's not even noon yet."

I could tell they spent a lot of time together by the way they played off of and teased each other, sometimes even finished each other's sentences as they talked. "No wonder," Stephanie, one of the paramedics, said. "We practically live together out here. We know each other's spouses, each other's kids."

"We're a tight-knit group," Fred said. "I mean, we tick each other off all the time, but we get over it. You can't hold a grudge on this job. No way. We depend on each other just like the person on the other end of the call is depending on us. When those tones go off, we go into what your sister calls EMS mode."

I asked her to explain what she meant by that as she scurried back and forth between the file cabinet and her desk. "They transform," she said and gestured toward them. "As you can clearly see, they are a bunch of goofballs. But when those tones go off," she snapped her fingers, "it's like Superman coming out of the phone booth. They are professional, focused, and instantly on top of the situation. I hope I never need them in that way, but if I do, I would trust them completely."

"Alright," someone groaned, "who paid her to say that?"

Kelly, another paramedic, pointed out that working for a small-town ambulance service was unique in that you knew most of the people you were called out to help. You grew up around them or might even be related to them.

"So," I said, getting a great idea for another story, "you might get called out to save the bully who pushed you around in school?" They laughed and shrugged, "It could happen, sure, but it wouldn't matter; you'd set that aside and do your job."

As I was getting ready to wind things up, I noticed a teddy bear in a glass case that overlooked the small room. It donned an EMS uniform and a pair of glasses that rested on the end of its nose. "That's there to remind us that Mits is still looking out for us," my sister said, as she clacked away at the computer. "Mits" was Mitsuko Shumaker, the former Director of Operations who worked here for 36 years before retiring and losing a battle with cancer this past January.

"The bear's outfit is made from the fabric of the last uniform she wore here. Her glasses always rode low on her nose just like that, too," she laughed, telling me how she remembered her always looking over the top of them when she talked to her. "Everyone here has a Mits story to tell."

"Get us started on the Mits' stories," someone shouted from the back room, "and you are going to need another tablet."

Between the two interviews, I heard a lot of those stories and many others as well, far more than I could ever include in a single column and more than enough insight to create my fictional character. So, thank you to all those working at SCCAS for your time, and even more, thank you for your service.

WAYWARD SON: TRAVELS AND REFLECTIONS

NIGHT WALKS

One of the most valuable gifts my parents gave me was a love and appreciation of walking. From as far back as I can remember, we went on Sunday hikes. (We still do.) It was never for the health benefits—though that turned out to be a nice bonus—but simply for the act itself. Regardless of where I'm living, you will find me walking in the woods, through a park, over the quiet sidewalks of a small town or the busy streets of a big city. It's something I enjoy with company or alone, in all seasons, and at any hour. In fact, one of my favorite times to walk is at night. The world comes alive in a very unique way when the sun goes down. Things look different, the senses sharpen, conversations and thoughts run deeper than usual, and the imagination is unleashed.

While I prefer rural or country hikes, this applies to any nighttime walk. When I was living in DC, for example, I took a date to see the monuments at night. Even though she and I had both seen them at least half a dozen times on our own, with friends, or as a tour guide for people who came to visit us, it was a completely different experience at night. (I actually fictionalized this experience in a later chapter of *A Noble Story*.)

Since I have been back in Clarion County, I've taken advantage of going out often. The other night, I met my dad and my sister, Jeanne, at her house for one of these hikes. It was a typical late fall evening—chilly, but not cold—and just right if you wore a heavy sweatshirt and kept moving. We planned what would be an average length hike for us, a five-mile circle that would take us to and through Sligo, and then back to Jeanne's house where we started. Thanks to a star-filled sky and the glow of a nearly full moon, we never needed to turn on the flashlights we had brought with us. Often times on these outings, a car would come along and stop to ask if we needed a lift, assuming we'd broken down somewhere. When we'd tell them thanks, we were just out for a stroll, we'd usually get a strange look and sometimes an "ah...okay?" before they drove off.

That night, though, the dirt roads we traveled were vacant and the only sound echoing through the dark woods were our footsteps, our voices, and laughter as we caught each other up on the events of the past week. When the conversation lulled, there was no hurry to fill the space because the silence of the evening was in itself a thing to behold and enjoy.

Most of Sligo was asleep by the time we got there. Walking up Bald Eagle Street, Dad reminisced about his childhood and adolescence here, pointing out the long-gone places—the movie theater, Rosie's restaurant, the hardware store, the service station, the drug store—that once populated what was and still is the main drag of the town. Something about the quietness of the night and the crisp autumn air charged my imagination and I could see it as it must have looked in the 1950s, with the old cars, the way people dressed, and my father as a child looking up at the rack of comic books in the back of the drug store while slurping down a fountain Coke bought with a hard-earned nickel.

Jeanne and I shared our memories of Saturdays spent at Grandma Drayer's, making the trek to Paul's Market like it was a great adventure where we'd buy penny candy or a bottle of Yoo-hoo, which we referred to as "chocolate pop."

With all the talk of snacks and drinks, we couldn't leave Sligo without stopping off at the Citgo for something to nibble on and a hot beverage to go with it. Which brings up another perk of these ventures: everything tastes better when consumed on a night walk. (If you don't believe me, test the theory for yourself.)

It was surprising how quickly we'd covered the five miles. There was still so much to talk about. But we said our goodbyes, went to our separate homes and lives and knew we'd sleep well that night. It was an excellent way to spend an evening.

Still, I feel I should offer a word of caution: night hikes do have a very real element of danger to them, which is one of the reasons I believe the senses are heightened when walking at night; it's the body's natural defenses kicking up a notch. While I have never had anything truly bad happen through the years, I have tripped over things I didn't see, had passing cars get a little too close, and once, I even had an overzealous old man with a gun think I was a terrorist. So, do be careful. Nothing ruins a great night hike like getting hit by a car or getting shot by a guy who thinks he's Clint Eastwood.

That being said, if you've never taken a night hike, I highly recommend it.

YOUR BEST SHOT

If you see me around town looking crazed, wound-up, spaced-out, and talking to myself—I mean, more than usual—don't be alarmed. I am participating in this year's National Novel Writing Month (aka NaNoWriMo), where every November, participants commit to writing a 50,000-word novel in 30 days. Yes, you read that correctly: I am attempting to write a 50,000-word novel in the month of November. There is no entry fee and the challenge is open to anyone who wants to give it a shot, from first-time writers to best-selling authors. Novels can be written on any subject and in any language. This year, over 300,000 people from more than 200 countries have signed up.

Diving into situations where I am in over my head is nothing new for me. I once fasted for a week to see what I could learn from it, applied for and got several jobs that I was ridiculously under-qualified for, and moved to a city (two cities, actually) that I'd never even visited prior to relocating because there was an opportunity there if I acted quickly. Sometimes these ventures were wildly successful. Other times, they were miserable failures. But every time, I walked away having learned something valuable that I would have never known had I not put myself out there.

Living by the seat of your pants isn't for everyone, I know, but I do think everyone can benefit by stepping out of their comfort zone from time to time, pushing themselves to do something they've always wanted to do but for whatever reason, wouldn't let themselves try. Challenging yourself like this wakes you up, shows you what you're made of, gives you the opportunity to make adjustments in your life, and win or lose, kicks your confidence up a notch or two.

Personally, I tend to go for the big thrills, but these individual challenges can be anything: a routine of walking three times a week, learning to play your favorite song on the guitar by your birthday, running a 5k race, organizing a community fundraiser, taking a class in something you've always been interested in, losing x amount of weight by swimsuit season, or taking a trip somewhere you've always wanted to go. The main thing is that it is something that you really want, so much so that you will keep working to make it happen even if the outlook is bleak.

Just as the adage says, you don't know what you can do until you try. Therefore, I suggest attempting something you are going to have to work at, really stretch to reach. It should be something that is very doable but will take a solid and sustained effort. If you have been on autopilot for a while, you will hit your first obstacles right away and then your fears and doubts will be staring you in the face, maybe even screaming in your face. This is actually a good thing if you can stay cool and observe what's happening, what you're feeling, why you are shutting down, getting angry, feeling sad or depressed, telling yourself that you are the biggest loser in recorded history. Just take a breath and look at it, acknowledge it, and keep right on moving forward.

The thing about doubts and fears is that everyone has them. Everyone. Knowing what yours are and where they are coming from is one of the real benefits of challenging yourself. Once you know what they are, you can make adjustments to overcome or compensate for them.

Once again, this is where the journey proves to be more important than the destination. It is during the struggle that you find your real strengths and learn how to overcome your weaknesses. For example: Guess how much money I will win if I succeed in this herculean task of writing a 50,000-word novel in a month. None. Guess what magazines will do a write up on me if I hit my average of 1,667 words a day, every day, for the entire month. None. Prizes? Some discounts from sponsors of the event. That's it. And the same goes for every one of the other 300,000 people around the world giving it a shot.

So, why do it? There are as many different reasons as there are participants. Statistics show that 90 percent of those taking part in National Novel Writing Month will fail to hit their goal, but most of them will be back next November to give it another try, because through just giving it their best shot, they probably got more words on the page in that single month than they did in the entire year. And they couldn't help but learn a thing or two about themselves along the way.

As for me, I can't be certain that I will hit the goal—though I am still very much in the running—but I can guarantee that I will fight to the end. And if I haven't hit my word count by the 30th, I know I will be tapping away at the keyboard right up until the very last second ticks off the clock.

Visit nanowrimo.org for more information about National Novel Writing Month.

...an
...ck.
...ary
...like
...ust,
...ness
...Mus-
...tivals

...just returned...
...also pleased to have...
mountaineers and...
US and UK. It was
together in Musso...

trut|

BAD NEWS

I am convinced that paying too much attention to the news can be hazardous to your health. The barrage of inexcusable violence, political madness, and gut-wrenching misery in the last month alone is enough to make anyone pop a spring. And thanks to cable news and social media, we can binge on it around the clock. I recently overdosed on the news, and the result was not pretty. The first symptoms were high levels of anger and frustration, which led to strange behavior. For instance, I found myself yelling at the television while pacing a hole in the living room floor. Then, though no one was asking, I was annoying friends and family with impassioned lectures on what was wrong with the world today and what I think we need to do to fix it. These pontifications were completely irrational and uncharacteristically peppered with expletives, leaving my audience looking disturbed and concerned for my well-being. Then came the second symptom, which was the hopeless feeling that I might as well just jump off the highest bridge I can find.

I wouldn't actually do that, of course, because it would be a bummer for my loved ones and put a real damper on the holiday season. All that time and effort and thought put into decorating the house, buying presents, planning meals...ruined. I couldn't do that to them, nor could I do that to myself. Despite our imperfect world, I generally enjoy the holidays and definitely don't want to miss out on the all the delicious food and revelry! Besides, the solution to changing my state of mind required no medication, no change in diet, or upgraded exercise program: I simply had to turn off the news.

While this resolution was simple, it was not easy. I went through withdrawal at first. I felt anxious, like something extremely important and unimaginably terrible was happening in the world and I was out of the loop. The whole planet was in imminent danger, and

I was in the dark because I had recklessly shut off the news! I was ready to turn the television back on, arm myself with the horrible knowledge of what was going on in the world and hear who was saying what so I could...so I could...what?

Yell at the television and pace the floor? Frighten everyone with another speech? Start scoping out bridges? No. I resolved to stick to the plan and stay away from the news for at least two weeks.

What happened next was weird. First of all, the world did not stop turning. The sun came up in the morning, and then at the end of the day, it went down again. My head started to clear. Instead of being told what was happening in the world, who I should hate, who hated me, and what horrible things were going to happen any minute now, I put my focus on what I was experiencing in my life first-hand.

A steady diet of the news had left me feeling that nothing I did made a difference at all. Going out into the day and interacting with the people around me proved that theory wrong. Think I'm blowing smoke at you? Talking all pie in the sky? Test it. Next time you are out, try different methods of approaching people and notice how your actions make a difference in how your day unfolds.

For example, open the door for someone with their arms full of packages, give a stranger or an acquaintance a genuine compliment, look the cashier in the eye during your transaction, treat people in a friendly manner. This works in the other direction as well. You can also shove past the person with the packages and let the door slam in their face, genuinely insult that stranger or acquaintance, roll your eyes at the cashier when they tell you the price of your items, and purposely be rude every chance you get. Either line of behavior will change the course of your day, though with the latter, you will probably not be as pleased with the outcome and you could very well get into a fistfight.

The point is that our individual lives and choices still make a difference and too much time gazing at a newscaster with horrific pictures flashing by makes it very easy to forget that. One of the things I have always valued—in myself and in others—is individuality, that ability to be who you are, walk to the beat of your own drum, regardless of who does or doesn't agree with you. The news has a tendency to categorize us, lump us into groups—liberals and conservatives, whites and blacks, this religion and that, on and on—until individual faces and names disappear. Once everyone is in their assigned group and pitted against each other, the inevitable fighting breaks out. Then it is *show time!* The bigger the fight, the bigger the story.

I once dated a reporter who worked for a national newspaper and thinking of all this, I am reminded of a newsroom maxim she once shared with me: If it bleeds, it leads.

Well, that explains a lot and keeping that in mind is a good way to maintain perspective. While it is important to stay informed, there is no need to pop a spring or jump off a bridge.

PUSH-OPEN
2CH
M1
M2
STEREO
NICAM DIGITAL STEREO
SUPER 4-HEAD
VHS
PLAY
REC
REMOTE CONTROL UNIT
MEMORY/ REPEAT/SEARCH
REV/PLAY
RESET/ INDEX
STILL ADV
VTR
CLOCK/ COUNTER
AUDIO OUT
REC
STOP
PLAY
SEARCH
PAUSE/STILL

OLD FAVORITES

'T is the season to revisit old movies. Whether these are dramas like *It's a Wonderful Life* or *Miracle on 34th Street,* or comedies such as *Home Alone, Elf,* or *National Lampoon's Christmas Vacation,* for a lot of people, the holidays aren't complete without these or other Christmas classics. Re-watching our favorites, however, is not limited to any one season or type of movie, but is a practice many people—myself included—engage in year round. While I will never lose my appetite for a great new film, there is no substitute for relaxing with one that I know inside out and have a real history with. I find that sitting down with an old favorite works as a kind of gauge of both where I am and where I've been.

I recently realized that I crave these most when I am not feeling well. If I am in bed with the flu or feeling down about something, these are the ones I want to watch. This struck me. If I was laid up in bed, why wouldn't I want to be entertained by something new and different? Why would I want to watch something I had already seen before, where I knew exactly what was going to happen and could even quote half of the lines?

Because, I believe, these old favorites offer us comfort.

In my last column, I wrote about watching the news and feeling like the world was in utter chaos and everyone seemed to be losing their minds. Yet, when I turn to one of these movies that I love and know well, I find there is order. Every film has its own reality, and it is a reality I know and understand. I can count on it. I know that certain actions are going to lead to specific reactions. It makes sense. At the beginning of one of my all-time favorites— *Rocky,* for example—I know the hapless boxer is "a bum" and "ain't never had any luck" in life, but I also know he's going to get a rare opportunity and as difficult as it may be, he is going to give it everything he has.

Because I know the movie so well, I don't have to work hard at paying attention. I can even drift off for a few minutes, lying there in bed with the flu, because when I wake up, I will know right where Rocky is and right where he's heading. *Rocky*—and I am speaking of only the first in the series here—has a lot of grit and realism about it. But it doesn't take me away from reality so much as it grounds me and reminds me of the characteristics I admire and aspire to.

Watching these films with others is usually a lot of fun. Every time I share one with someone, I come across something that I have never noticed before, no matter how many times I've seen it. And the experience is especially satisfying when they like the movie as much as I do.

This doesn't always happen. Sometimes the other person simply doesn't share your enthusiasm. Maybe they don't really get the movie the way you do, or worse—they don't like it at all. This can be awkward. As I write this, I am reminded of such an occasion and feel compelled to pass it along. A couple of years ago, I was going out with a woman who also had a collection of movies that she would re-watch on a somewhat regular basis. When we realized this, we were excited to share with each other. The first two movies she showed me—obscure art films I'd never heard of and don't remember the names of—had no dialogue at all. They were told purely through imagery. Not my cup of tea, but I watched them and looked for things I could appreciate. I saw some very impressive cinematography and we discussed that.

Then it was my turn. I knew trouble was brewing when she kept making fun of the 1970s hairstyles and clothing in *Rocky* instead of paying attention to the characters and their struggles. This was annoying, but we weren't in real danger until we got to the second movie: *Cool Hand Luke*. She didn't like Paul Newman's rebellious, unbreakable character, and instead, identified more with the prison guards and the sadistic warden who tried to break him. I have to admit that I got to see a couple of my favorite films from a new and different perspective, and to me at least, they held up well. That relationship, sadly, did not.

Then again, maybe it's not sad. Sharing our movie choices made our fundamental differences clear and probably saved us a lot of frustration by speeding up our inevitable parting. Maybe finding a woman I have favorite movies in common with is the way to go. Maybe she's somewhere out there right now watching one of them.

Who knows? If that's the case, my old favorites not only tell me where I am and where I've been, but may very well foreshadow where I'm heading next.

GREAT EXPECTATIONS

It is the first week of 2016 and one of the very few Januarys in my adult life where I am not struggling under the weight of New Year's resolutions. I decided to skip the annual ritual this year. It all started when—in hopes of gathering material for this column—I asked a number of people what their resolutions were for the new year. I was met with a lot of groaning and eye-rolling. "It's a bunch of bologna," a guy told me. "The only difference between December 31st and January 1st is a tick of the clock. People make too dang much of it." One woman said she didn't believe in making resolutions anymore because she knew from past experience that life would get in the way, she would fall short of reaching her goals, and end up feeling bad about herself. Her husband backed her up, nodding and waving the subject away. "Too much pressure." Even those who did voice their hopes did so half-heartedly. "Well, I wouldn't mind losing this gut," they'd say, or, "It would be nice to get out of debt," but it was clear they didn't have much of a plan in place or really expect it to happen.

I've been hearing these sentiments more often over the past few years and was wondering if the long tradition of New Year's resolutions had become nothing more than a form of self-harassment, a practice that had run its course and become obsolete. It is no secret, after all, that the vast majority of people don't hit their goals. Some don't even make it to February. I know I didn't hit mine last year and, yeah, I felt bad about it. Considering all this, I decided to take it easy on myself this year, just coast along, let the days unfold as they may. No lofty goals. No big plans. No pressure.

And, man, have I been bored.

I know it has only been a week, but that's been ample time for me to miss the annual challenge. Skipping the tradition this year has made me look deeper into it and understand why it is important to pledge some kind of self-improvement in the upcoming year and why it has been a custom in different cultures and communities for centuries. While humanity is rife with faults and weaknesses, one of our undeniable strengths is an innate desire to progress, to actively evolve, and go further than those that came before us. That drive doesn't only exist in the species as a whole, but also in most of us individually. I believe it springs not from what we are lacking, but from an instinctual fascination with what is possible, what might be attainable if we're willing to reach for it.

That is what I am missing and why I've decided to change my mind about skipping the resolutions this year. The line between December 31st and January 1st may be imaginary, but I believe it is there for a reason. For one thing, life goes by quickly and if we're not marking the passage from one year to the next, taking the time to reflect on the previous year and lay out plans to be better next year, it would go even faster and it would be difficult to give our lives much in the way of direction.

So, maybe rather than abandoning the practice, I would suggest that people alter their approach somewhat. Try lowering the bar a bit and instead of shooting for one big goal for the year, break it down into small achievements along the way. For example, pay off a credit card by May and another one by October instead of trying to pay everything off by the end of the year.

The commitment is important too. When I think of the times I was most successful—those years I took the trip to Europe, got in shape, wrote that book—there was nothing half-hearted about my approach. A resolution, after all, is not a wistful dream, but a promise to yourself or someone else to do something so you have to plan for and expect success.

So, what do you really want from this year? What can you do to get it?

As soon as I send this column off, I am going to break out a pen and paper and answer those questions for myself. Why not? It's not that late of a start. The year is young; there are still 51 weeks to play with. If you didn't set any resolutions this year, why don't you join me? And if you did, good luck on staying the course.

Either way, I wish you a happy, healthy, and prosperous new year!

WAYWARD SON: TRAVELS AND REFLECTIONS

A LONG WALK

It is 11 degrees outside—much colder than forecasted—when I park the car in Lawsonham along the Redbank Valley Trail and start heading east with the intention of hiking until I am all hiked-out. Something I will definitely be able to accomplish because, from here, the trail follows the Redbank Creek through St. Charles, Climax, New Bethlehem, Hawthorn, Summerville—all the way to Brookville—which from where I am starting, is approximately 35 miles. I suppose this might seem a strange thing to do considering it is freezing outside, I barely slept at all last night, and I am behind on several fast-approaching deadlines. (Actually, it might appear a strange thing to do, period.) But believe it or not, this is my best chance at getting some sleep tonight, hitting those deadlines in the next couple of days, and not losing my mind in the process. The fact is that there are very few things in life that can clear my head, energize my body, and give me a sense of perspective like a long walk in the woods of western Pennsylvania.

So, here I am. I pull my hat down over my ears and shove my hands deep in my pockets, puffing steam, imagining the locomotives that once churned along this same route burning and transporting coal. A light coat of snow covers the ground and the trail stretches out before me, clean and undisturbed. The only sound is the steady rush of the Redbank Creek shimmering below. The gray trees and brown brambles on either side of the trail are sugar-coated with a heavy layer of frost. Icicles hang off the jagged rocks to my left, everything sparkling in the morning sun. I go at a good clip, trying to get warm while burning off the frantic energy that's been building for the last few weeks.

I don't know if it is the exercise, the fresh air, or just the magic of the forest, but the chattering to-do lists looping through my head have finally gone quiet and I am enjoying the silence. The only sounds I hear are my footfalls in the snow and the occasional burst of a grouse launching itself into flight. While I haven't seen any other wildlife so far, the tracks of deer, rabbit, raccoon, turkey, and others I cannot positively identify assure me that they are all here.

In about an hour, I am at the Long Point tunnel. The year 1898 is stamped on the keystone, faded but still readable. The entrance of brick and large stone extends about 30 feet. Past that, the air is damp with the smell of dirt and rock. Shining my flashlight upward reveals how the tunnel was carved out of solid rock, its rough and craggy surface stained black from the passage of countless trains.

Beyond the tunnel, I notice that the temperature has gone up considerably and with the steady pace, I haven't been cold since I left the car. I spot a huge rock along the creek that I used to visit as a kid, more years ago than I care to count. Shimmying down the hillside, slipping and sliding over the frozen, snow-covered ground to the water's edge, I find the rock just as I left it so long ago. I climb up on to it and enjoy an apple, a hunk of cheese, and a bottle of water I brought along. Lulled by the comforting rush of the creek while scanning the wooded hillside, I think about how the woods have always been my sanctuary, how they have never let me down.

This would probably be a good time to turn around, but I want to keep going and I know two people that would pick me up if I called them for a ride, so on I go. The trail winds and bends, offering some spectacular views. On a map or from an airplane, this route must look like a long, squiggly line. I remember walking various pieces of this trail with friends and family over the years, many of those trips back when the tracks were still in the ground. It is strange how I can still remember some of those distant conversations, my memory usually sparked by the landmarks along the way. Like, for example, how the deserted fire brick company in St. Charles reminds me of my dad telling me how he used to make the dies that they used to make the bricks. Or, approaching the Climax tunnel as I am now, and telling a friend how the entrance of the tunnel looked like that of an amusement park fun house. The icicles hanging down from the opening formed the long, pointy teeth of a giant, open mouth, promising scares and thrills to all those who dare to enter.

I have been going for several hours at this point and am ready to call it a day, but I can't be more than a couple of miles from New Bethlehem where, on Broad Street, I know I could find a hot meal and a cold brew. That thought settles it. I am pushing on to New Bethlehem.

HEADS UP

Recently, someone asked me if I was superstitious. I told them I was not. Then, later that day, I caught myself standing over two pennies on the ground while I was putting gas in my car. One was heads up, the other was tails up. Without even thinking about it, I picked up the one on heads, made a wish, and put it in my pocket. The other one? It's probably still there. The very next day at the coffee shop, I commented to the person in front of me on the mild winter we've been having here in western Pennsylvania this year—and then proceeded to nearly knock him over while lunging to knock on the wooden counter.

Okay, so maybe I am a little superstitious.

But why? Do I honestly believe that wishing on a heads-up penny will bring me the object of my desire, or that picking up the other one would bring bad luck my way? No, not really. Nor do I truly believe that commenting on the mild winter and then knocking on wood are going to change the weather patterns in the next couple of months. And yet, out of habit, human nature, or wishful thinking, odds are good that I will continue indulging in these behaviors.

Superstitions have been with us for thousands of years in some cases. Even though they have historically sprung from ignorance and fear, hanging on to these notions and performing these little rituals have become a kind of tradition or habit that we no longer bother to really think about, let alone question.

As a boy, I was fascinated with the story of the Titanic. The most luxurious ship in the world, considered unsinkable, and yet, down it went on its maiden voyage. I remember someone at school telling me it was because they had called it unsinkable. Imagining it disappearing into the deep, dark, icy waters with more than a thousand passengers aboard apparently made quite an impression on my young mind. If only they wouldn't have made such an arrogant claim, I thought, or at least remembered to knock on wood, the great ship would probably still be afloat.

That's not to say that superstitions weren't contested in my childhood. My dad claimed to be superstitious, but my mom was not. I remember him standing on a huge extension ladder while she walked under it—repeatedly—winking at us kids and laughing, while he kept shouting down at her to cut it out. She was also known to open umbrellas in the house and boldly pay no heed whatsoever to Friday the 13th. I don't recall any negative repercussions resulting from her daring disregard of these time-honored notions.

Still, they continue to endure.

I think this has a lot to do with human nature. Our lives are full of uncertainty and the world can be a very dangerous place, which makes us vulnerable. When things happen randomly, or for seemingly no reason, we feel helpless. Therefore, we are driven to try to understand why things happen and what we can do to maintain some kind of control of our lives. If we can't find a reason for why something is happening, we'll make one up! Being prepared for a job interview, a presentation, or a big game is the key factor, of course, but things could still go wrong. Donning a pair of lucky socks is that one extra step you can take to turn the tides of fate in your favor.

Now that I realize I am somewhat superstitious and have examined it a bit, I have noticed that, in my case, it has more to do with hope than anything else. Fear has never been a big motivator for me. I am much more likely to run after something I want than to run away from something I don't. While I don't put a lot of stock in astrology, I always take a peek at my horoscope if it is in a newspaper or a magazine I am reading. If it is something negative or lame, I tend to ignore it. If it is something positive, I will pay attention to it, even tear it out and stick it in my pocket sometimes. In planning the release date of my new novella, *Attachment*, I chose February 8th because it's the first day of the Chinese New Year, and this year—the year of the monkey—is supposed to be very lucky for my sign (the dragon) according to the Chinese zodiac.

Intellectually, I know releasing my book on the first day of the Chinese New Year will not guarantee huge book sales and wishing on a penny won't bring me the woman of my dreams, but emotionally, some part of me wants to believe it just might. It's certainly not hurting anything, and you know, I have a feeling these wishes are going to come true this year.

Knock on wood.

A DARK TUNNEL AND A
SUPERNATURAL TALE

My novella—*Attachment*—is being released today and I want to celebrate by hopping on the bike and getting lost in that state of mind motorcyclists live for, that feeling of freedom, that fusion of excitement and tranquility. However, it's freezing in the small, western Pennsylvania town where I am currently holed up and my bike is in storage until April.

So...the next best thing to an open-ended bike ride—believe it or not—is an open-ended hike and this time of year is as good as any to go. There is no shortage of woods and trails around here to lose myself in. I choose one that travels along what used to be the old Allegheny Valley Railroad founded in the 1850s. The train tracks are long gone, but the hiking trail follows its course alongside the Redbank Creek, featuring several tunnels and winding through 41 miles of forest, small towns, and villages in Armstrong, Clarion, and Jefferson counties.

I love the tunnels. They have this mysterious attraction. Especially when, like today, I am approaching one I've never been through before. I don't know how long it is, what kind of shape it is in, or how far I will have to brave the darkness before seeing the light at the other end. Stepping inside, I can't help but wonder what I'd do if I came upon something lurking inside...like a wounded, wild animal or a madman hiding out from the world.

This actually reminds me of the feeling I had when I sat down to write *Attachment*. The story of a man becoming possessed and steadily taken over by an angry disembodied spirit had been in my mind since the fall of 2012, but I avoided writing it. I told myself it was because the supernatural genre wasn't my thing, that the tale would be too long for a short story and too short for a novel, but the real reason I avoided it is because I know how deep I go into whatever world I write about and this one had the potential to be very dark.

I had almost forgotten about it when I started having nightmares a year ago. I could see the character of Paul very clearly in those creepy dreams. I don't want to give anything away, but let's just say he is not the kind of guy...or rather ghost...that is easily ignored. I knew I had to write the story then just like I have to walk through this dark tunnel now.

I barely slept during the time I wrote the early drafts and there were times when I felt like I do today as I get to that point in the middle of the tunnel where the light behind me disappears and I have yet to see any light at the other end.

But, as is often the case in life, I have found that if I keep moving forward, the light will appear and the story will unfold as it is supposed to.

LOOKING BACK

I visited my good friend in Pittsburgh last week. We'd first met in this city as undergraduates at Pitt over 25 years ago. Both of us were born in small western Pennsylvania towns and were eager to get out and see the world. Since then, we have each lived in many different cities across the country, and in his case, even abroad. While waiting for his girlfriend to join us, we drank Manhattans, talked about the experiences of the past two and a half decades, and marveled at how quickly the time had passed. Shortly after our third party arrived, the conversation took a philosophical turn and that age-old question came up: if you could go back in time and do it all again, would you?

I am not sure if any of us actually answered the question, as merely pondering it spun the discussion in countless other directions (fueled by the Manhattans). I have since revisited the subject and concluded that if I could go back with the knowledge I have gained over the years and be able to apply it, then a do-over would be great. I'd know what I was doing this time around and would be able to avoid most of the pitfalls and difficulties I'd encountered. However, if I had to go back and re-learn all those lessons again, repeat the same mistakes, and suffer the same wounds, I'd probably pass.

This surprised me. Did I have that many regrets? Well, no, not really. Sure, if I had it to do over again, I would have stayed in touch with that small-time playwright who went on to become a rich and famous movie producer, talked to that mysterious, beautiful woman in Nashville instead of just exchanging smiles, and I would never have gone into business with that company in California when I knew in my gut they couldn't be trusted. But overall, I have more to be grateful for than to mourn over. And so, in that spirit, rather than dwell on the things I regret, I'd like to take a moment to focus on the things I am glad I did do, the things I will never feel sorry for. Here are some of them:

Taking a trip. I love to travel, and over the years, have had many chances to do so. However, almost every single time the opportunity presented itself, my first response was that I didn't have the time or the money to go. Thankfully, I always went anyway and was never disappointed.

Exercising. While I work out pretty regularly, I am rarely thrilled at the prospect of doing it. Still, I am always glad afterward. Not only is there a sense of accomplishment, but it feels great when the blood is pumping and the endorphins are firing. I have never returned from a brisk hike or walked out of the gym saying, "Man, I wish I would have stayed on the couch eating Doritos."

Apologizing. This one is no fun at all. It is hard to do, but if I know I have done something wrong or have hurt someone—intentionally or not—I try to apologize. Regardless of how the other person reacts, it makes me feel better. (Plus, the times I didn't apologize when I knew I should have ended up haunting me for years.)

Giving a compliment. I don't do this unless I really mean it because it doesn't work otherwise. But when I see someone who stands out in some way, who is really good at something, or goes that extra mile, I make it a point to let them know that I noticed, that someone appreciates their talent or effort. If I am admiring it anyway, why not let them know? It costs me nothing and might make their day.

Telling someone you love them when you really do. Okay, this is getting a little mushy, but I have to include it because it is probably the most important one on the list. I have never regretted doing this. It is harder for some people than others, but it is too important to just assume they know.

Going for it. Chasing after something I have always wanted or dreamed of achieving is worth the ride. When I succeeded, it was a terrific feeling, a special kind of high. But even when I didn't get what I went after, or the whole enterprise turned out to be a bust, it was still worth taking the chance. As much as I hated falling on my face or getting slammed to the ground, I've never had to wonder "what if?" and I knew that when I got back up each time, I'd be tougher than I was when I was knocked down.

Riding my motorcycle. Yes, I know it is dangerous, but riding gives me a feeling of freedom and excitement like nothing else. I don't take the risks lightly, but I accept them as part of the deal.

I'm sure I could think of others, but I'm out of column space. So, what about you? Did any of these resonate? I suggest that you take a few minutes to look back over your life and think about the things you're glad you did, and hopefully, continue to do.

Go ahead. You won't regret it.

NEW DIRECTIONS

Following your gut is a no-brainer.

Because, oftentimes, if you really think about what it's telling you to do, you might not do it. And no wonder. Instincts aren't based on reason and sometimes can even appear illogical. Four years ago, while working in a corporate office in the DC Metro area, I remember staring out the window and fantasizing about what it would be like to hand in my notice, get on my motorcycle, and go wherever the road took me.

Just like that, I knew this would be the subject of my next novel. I didn't do market research or ask around to see what others thought of the idea. I simply got to work. I spent the whole following year writing that book—*A Noble Story*—and the year after that working to get it published. Once it was slated for publication, I had another intuitive flash. This one much more dramatic, telling me it was time to leave DC and ... do it in style.

So, I handed in my notice, took off on my motorcycle, and went wherever the road took me.

It wasn't quite as easy as it sounds and a lot scarier, but it was great. As you know, I eventually ended up here in Clarion County where I got an apartment, started writing the next book, and enjoyed lots of time with my family. Now, after being here for over a year—it's hard to believe I have been writing this column for 15 months!—something is telling me it is time to pull up stakes and head on to the next place.

Yikes! Part of me wants to pretend I didn't get the memo, but in the past, ignoring my instincts has proven to be a bad idea. Years ago, when I was in LA trying to break into the movie business, I found an agency that loved my work and was sure they could sell my screenplays for big bucks. This was great because I didn't have a single contact in LA and no one would even return a call, let alone read one of my scripts. I was thrilled ... until I sat down with the owner of the company.

There was something I didn't like about him, something that felt shady. My gut told me he couldn't be trusted and I should say thanks, but no thanks, and be on my way. But I had no logical reason for distrusting him. The company's credentials checked out and he said all the right things, knew all the right people. I didn't know a soul in the business, had no other offers at the time and was flat broke. This agency was promising to be my ticket in and all I had to do was sign.

Colossal mistake. They never got me a single meeting or sold a word of my work, but because of the contract I'd signed, they demanded 15 percent of anything I made as a writer for the duration of our agreement, which included the writing gigs that I'd gotten myself and was barely surviving on. (Total bonehead move on my part for not having a lawyer go over it first, but I was young and naïve. I eventually got out of that mess and never made that mistake again.) The point is that I knew unconsciously that they were crooked, but at the time, a suspicious feeling wasn't a good enough reason for me to walk away, so I stepped right into a trap.

Ever since then, when I get a hunch like that, good or bad, I take it seriously. The tough part is that they usually show up un-beckoned and unannounced, coming out of nowhere. Nevertheless, there are a couple of things I have found to be helpful in encouraging that sixth sense. First of all, if a person or a situation elicits a response in me, logical or not, I take note and don't rationalize it away. Oddly, I have seen dogs do this with strangers. They may like one person and not another even though both people treat them the same way. Dogs don't argue with their instincts and I guess humans shouldn't either.

The best tactic, however, for rousing that kind of insight is to unplug on a somewhat regular basis, especially when you are trying to make a major decision. No phone, no email, no Internet, no television—nothing external. Go out into the woods and sit by a stream, or find a quiet place surrounded by trees. Breathe deep. Relax. Chill out until the inner chatter dies down. Do this once a week and before you know it, you will actually be able to hear yourself think.

In fact, I am going to unplug right now and head out to the woods, see if I can get a feel for where I should head next. There will be one more *Tales of a Wayward Son* after this one. Then, I will be off towards ... well, whichever direction that internal compass points to.

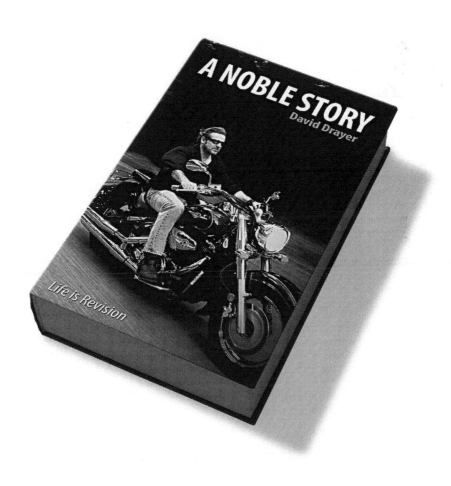

WAYWARD SON: TRAVELS AND REFLECTIONS

CROWN JEWELS

I announced in my last column that the wanderer in me was restless and ready to move on to the next adventure. A regular reader of *Wayward Son* responded by offering some kind words about the column, wishing me luck, and asking how I found the guts—though he used a more colorful expression—to just pick up, take off, and start over in a new place. "How do you know," he asked, "that you are doing the right thing?"

That got me to thinking about the many questions I have pondered in this column over the past 15 months while inviting you to join me on long hikes, family visits, and open-ended motorcycle trips. Knowing you were out there reading, considering these musings with me, I have asked to what end do we pursue the things we do in life, what we hold on to and let go of, what power there might be in New Year's resolutions, and what things we will never regret doing.

Therefore, it seems fitting to explore the question posed above. I took off on my first big adventure shortly after graduating Union High School and leaving Rimersburg many moons ago in a rusted-out Plymouth. I never got tired of taking off on a wish and a prayer as there was always some new place to experience and explore. But, back to the question: How do I know I am doing the right thing?

The short answer is ... I don't.

And I never really have. A hard fact of life I have had to accept over the years is that we never really know, not for sure, if we are making the best decisions or going in the right direction. To paraphrase the novelist, Milan Kundera, because we only get one life, we can't compare it with our other lives or apply what we've learned so far to our future ones. This is all we've got. This is it.

Which is kind of a bummer when you think about it.

Especially considering that our whole lives are full of these major decisions. No matter who you are or where you are in your life, I know you have been faced with an unending series of choices, be it taking a job, getting married, having kids, relocating, retiring, and on and on. Yet, none of us can really know for sure that we are making the best possible moves.

Now, before I become too much of a downer, I also have to say that I have come to realize that we can uncover some pretty good hints if we follow our instincts, use our heads, and muster up the courage to take action.

My life has been more unstructured than most, but I'm betting that the same things that worked for me in navigating my adventures will work for most people in most situations. One of the crown jewels for me has always been listening to and following my instincts. When I feel something pulling at me or nagging at me, I pay attention to it. By letting the noise in my head go quiet in the solitude of the woods or be drowned out by the steady thrumming of my motorcycle, I can count on a gut feeling or a flash of insight to give me a good clue as to what I need to do next.

Likewise, I have learned to use my head, but not to overuse it. No matter what you're doing nowadays, the Internet makes it easy to get more information on any subject than you could ever need to make a good decision. The old pros and cons list is still a good staple when trying to reach an answer or determine a new direction as is considering different scenarios: best case, worst case, and most likely.

That's all using your head, but if it goes on too long, you run the risk of thinking something to death. When gathering information and thinking everything out turns into dilly-dallying, constant flipping and flopping back and forth, it's time to stop thinking and make a move. Otherwise, you won't do anything. This is paralysis through analysis.

To avoid this fate, give yourself a reasonable deadline and stick to it. If you reach the deadline and still can't decide, flip a coin. The important thing at this point is that you make a decision and go with it. While I have reverence for the incredible power of words, actions will always speak louder.

Which is where I am now: ready for the next adventure, not a hundred percent sure that I am doing the right thing, but with some pretty decent hints suggesting that I am. Either way, I'm going for it.

Hopefully, I will have the opportunity to return with a guest piece once in a while from wherever I land next. Until then, know that writing this column for *The Leader-Vindicator* has been a real pleasure. My friends, I hope you enjoyed it as much as I did.

LILY DALE THE TOWN
THAT TALKS TO THE DEAD

They say "getting there is half the fun" and on a motorcycle, it is typically a lot more than half. But today isn't typical. An un-forecasted rainstorm has me stranded (unpleasantly) in Pleasantville, Pennsylvania, on my way to Lily Dale, New York, also known as "the town that talks to the dead."

I first heard of Lily Dale a few years ago when I was living in DC and dating a woman who was into the paranormal. I was intrigued to learn that the small, upstate community has been attracting people attempting to contact the other side for more than 150 years. A *New York Times* article referred to it as a place that draws the "intellectually curious and the emotionally vulnerable," summoning "visionaries and fools" hoping to commune with the dead. While I have no burning desire to chat with the departed and wouldn't call myself a visionary or a fool, I am definitely curious.

On second thought, maybe I am a fool, sitting here at a diner in Pleasantville, soaking wet, nursing a fourth cup of coffee, and watching the rain assault my motorcycle. The storm hit about six or seven miles from here, just outside of Tionesta on a stretch of road that offered no shelter, not even a decent place to pull off. This was particularly annoying because I always carry raingear on extended trips but the storm came up so suddenly that I was soaked before I could get to it.

I check the forecast between here and Lily Dale on my laptop for the umpteenth time and it is still vague, saying basically, that it *may* continue to rain throughout the day...and then again, it *may not* continue to rain throughout the day. The logical thing to do in this situation is call the trip off, head for home, and reschedule. However, the main attractions in Lily Dale are seasonal and that season ends in the next two days. Rescheduling means waiting until next year, which I'd rather not do.

Outside, the downpour has dwindled to a light rain but doesn't look like it is going to stop anytime soon. If this were a bar instead of a diner, I'd be tempted to order a few fingers of Jameson, find a nearby motel, and call it a day. But since it is not a bar and the rain has slowed down enough to make riding possible, I am going to continue heading north.

The rain stops by the time I cross the New York state line. It stays away until I am a half-hour from my destination and another downpour forces me into another diner.

I finally pull up to Lily Dale's gated entrance much later than expected and with a good-sized headache, but thankful to have made it in one piece. The girl in the booth explains the daily and weekly passes while I locate my wallet under the rain suit. It's still sodden with the morning's storm and I hand her two soggy bills—a 5 and a 10—for a 24-hour pass. She hesitates and I say, "It's just rain. Not sweat or anything disgusting." She takes the bills gingerly and we both start to laugh.

Cruising up and down the quiet streets, I pass some grand Victorian houses, but the majority of the residents live in small, modest homes, many sporting a colorful shingle in the front yard with the name and phone number of the medium or spiritual advisor who lives there. There are community buildings, a church, a museum, a gift shop, a café, a couple of parks, and a nice view of Cassadaga Lake.

From my research, I recognize a Victorian style building with a dozen rocking chairs lining its front porch as the Maplewood Hotel, which first opened its doors in 1880 and is allegedly haunted. I stop to see if I can get a room. The floorboards creak under my boots. I can feel the history of the place; it is like walking into another time.

"You look like you could use a room," a woman with long, gray hair says as I approach the front desk.

"And a hot shower," I add. She says she can't help me with that as there are only bathtubs available. "That will work," I say and she gives me the lowdown on the hotel like she is trying to get the bad news out of the way first. Many of the rooms share a bathroom and there is no air conditioning, no elevator, no television, and the nearest access to laundry facilities are in the next town over. I am low-maintenance by nature and even after the grueling ride here, I'm more interested in old world charm than the standard creature comforts. I do, however, prefer a private bath and manage to get one. She tells me to come to the front desk if I need anything—no phones here either—and hands me a key, a map of Lily Dale, and points out a dry erase board that lists the events for the rest of the day and evening. I don't know what a "Thought Exchange" is but it sounds worth checking out as does the "Ghost Walk" which will be held after dark.

My 3rd floor room is small for a double, but plenty for me. Before I even unpack, I start filling the claw foot tub with hot water and get out of my wet clothes. Each of the twin beds has a white bath towel fashioned into the shape of ... I'm going to guess a rabbit ... leaning against the headboard, holding a washrag and a travel-sized bar of soap. The bath feels good, encouraging my muscles to relax, the headache to lift, and my eyelids to get heavy.

It is somewhere around 10:00 at night and I am sitting on a wet bench in the middle of an old growth forest inside of Lily Dale, known as the Leolyn Woods. A heavy layer of clouds block the light of the moon and stars; the only sound is that of the occasional raindrop falling through trees. This is the last stop on the ghost walk, and at the request of our tour guides, we have shut off our flashlights and phones. It is so dark that I can't see the two dozen or so others sitting around me. I can't hear them either as we are supposed to be meditating. We are at a spot where spiritual contact regularly occurs and are encouraged, if we wish, to silently invite a deceased loved one to make their presence known.

I'm not convinced that such a thing is possible, but the unknown is so vast that I'm not ruling it out. This is the kind of strange and interesting event I was expecting to experience when I arrived, and for the past seven hours, I have not been disappointed. What I was not expecting was the tranquility of the place. Even sitting here in the middle of a dark forest asking the dead to speak doesn't feel as creepy as it should. Residents and visitors are friendly, easy to talk to. Earlier, I met a retired couple who came from Seattle in a motor home, a group of college girls on a road trip from Alfred University, and a woman who makes the trip from New Jersey every year.

Like the best ghost walks, this one has been more of a history lesson than anything else. The two-hour walk from one end of Lily Dale to the other has covered its evolution from a camp where free-thinkers and Spiritualists gathered to its incorporation in 1879 and its current status as one of the largest Spiritualist communities in the world. Also noted were the many famous people who visited

here, including Susan B. Anthony, whose radical notion that men and women were equal found an audience here. She spoke several times in Lily Dale, applauding Spiritualism as one of the only religious groups that practiced equality.

That's not to say that some of the history here didn't send a chill down my spine. For example, the "precipitated spirit paintings" displayed throughout Lily Dale are said to have appeared on canvases during séances, without a paintbrush or the touch of a human hand. One of the strangest events of the evening occurred where the cottage of the Fox sisters used to stand. (The alleged communication between the young Fox girls and the spirit of a murdered peddler caused a nationwide stir in 1848. Their cottage was later moved here from Hydesville, NY, where it stood until it burned to the ground in 1955.) Anyway, the woman next to me took a picture, then nudged me and whispered, "Am I crazy or is there something weird about this picture." I looked at the screen and didn't see anything at first, then noticed what appeared to be the image of a human skull in the darkness just behind the tour guide. "That's what I thought," she said and asked our guide to have a look.

He saw it too as did a few others who gathered around for a look. Some were convinced it was a skull, others waved it off as merely a light cast by the flash of another camera and the product of the collective imagination of a group of people on a ghost walk.

The silence of the dark forest is broken by a voice—one of the tour guides—asking if anyone experienced anything during the mediation that they would like to share. Out of respect for the privacy of those who spoke up, I won't give specific details here, but I can say that one person claims to have felt the touch of his late wife and two others say they received a message, one from a father, the other from a friend. The flashlights and phones come back on. We are all thanked for attending and reminded of the outdoor services that will be held here tomorrow where mediums will be on hand to relay messages from beyond to those in attendance. Then, we all head out of the woods and back to our rooms or campsites. Some people are quiet and some are chatty. I walk with a small group of people also staying at the Maplewood and we end up hanging out on the porch for a while, talking, laughing, most expressing wonder at what they saw and heard while a few express their doubts.

I wake the next morning to a bright and warm day that promises to be excellent riding weather. If the Maplewood is haunted, I need to sleep in haunted hotels more often because, despite a small, lumpy bed, I slept better than I have in months. I go in search of breakfast and lay my jacket in the sun to dry.

Riding out of Lily Dale in the early afternoon, I am not sure what to make of my short visit, but I'm glad I came and will undoubtedly be turning it over in my mind for a while. As for where the road is taking me next, I am heading north, thinking Buffalo or Niagara Falls when I pass a vineyard. The smell of grapes baking in the sun gives me a better idea and I start heading east ... for the Finger Lakes.

ENJOYING THE RIDE

After writing my last regular *Wayward Son* column this past March, the plan was to write a guest piece six months down the road to say hello to the readers of this column and let you all know where I landed. What I did not consider back then is that here in September, I would not have landed anywhere yet, that I'd still be circling, unable to find the right combination of location and employment to touch down. I'm not complaining, well, not now anyway, though it was frustrating at first. Then I talked to a good friend about it who reminded me of the many times I've been in this position before, this sort of holding pattern or intermission between the last thing I did and the next thing I'm doing.

Rather than try to force a direction, she suggested, pointing out what did and didn't work in the past, the key was to chill out and simply let things unfold and develop naturally. That sounds great, I told her, but how am I supposed to do that? "Just enjoy the ride," she said.

That turned out to be good counsel, especially because, for me, that directive had a very literal translation: ride the motorcycle whenever possible. With the excellent weather we've had this year combined with my flexible schedule, it has been possible almost 100 percent of the time. You've probably seen me cruising down Main Street in Rimersburg or, for that matter, any of the small towns the Leader-Vindicator reaches as I've rumbled through all of them a time or two since March.

Taking the motorcycle instead of the car gave even the most mundane errands a splash of color. Going to the dentist is a little less dreadful and getting groceries is more fun. I have to get creative, of course, when it comes to fitting everything in a set of saddlebags and a backpack, but it's become a game, a challenge. I rarely have to make a second trip and if I do, so what! That just means another motorcycle ride and it provides some free entertainment to my neighbor who comes out on the porch when she hears me pull in to see what I am carrying on my back and what I pull out of those saddlebags: a rotisserie chicken, a 12-pack of Coke, a watermelon. She always grins and shakes her head when I walk back carrying the loot.

I've also been motorcycling to job interviews—even the ones far away are part of an extended bike trip—and I have found it to be an effective icebreaker. If the person interviewing me is a bike lover, we talk motorcycles; if not, we talk about my ride to the office, which always involves a roundabout series of backroads and interesting landscapes, which brings up one of the things I found the most enjoyable on my rides since March: the backroads.

Despite growing up here, there are so many roads I didn't know. I never realized how many different combinations of roads a person could take going from one town to the next. The number of ways you can drive out of Curllsville is impressive, and there must be a dozen routes to get to New Bethlehem from just about anywhere in Clarion County.

But also, I'm rediscovering the roads I do know and thinking, as I whip past the farms on 536 between Punxsutawney and Mayport or twist from Sligo to Knox via Canoe Ripple, how these roads tell the story of our lives. My grandparents used to live down that road, my first girlfriend on that street, and I can't cross the Lawsonham Bridge without remembering that just down the muddy path next to it is where I learned to swim. And when your western Pennsylvania roots run as deeply as mine on both my mom's and my dad's side of the family, that history includes your parents, grandparents, great-grandparents and beyond.

I'm running out of column space here, so let me end by mentioning just a couple of the fantastic day trips I have taken. I'm sure you know all about these, but let them serve as a reminder with October just around the corner: Benezette (go in late afternoon to see the most elk), Cook Forest and Clear Creek, or just get on Route 6 and go (especially for the foliage). This is just a start as there are countless great drives in every direction.

I'll check back in again—from where I don't know—at the end of the year.

WAYWARD SUN: TRAVELS AND REFLECTIONS

AWAKEN THE MUSE

The temperature is hovering around 45 degrees this morning with a projected high of 50 and the roads are wet from an all-night rain. Conventional wisdom would say this is *not* a motorcycle day despite the fact that I really need one. I have to write and submit a newspaper article by 5:00 this afternoon and all of my ideas seem to have gone to sleep or disappeared entirely. One of the beauties of freelancing is having the freedom to do whatever you need to do to jumpstart your brain and get things flowing again. For me, a motorcycle ride usually does the trick.

So, low temperatures, wet roads, and conventional wisdom be damned. I put on an extra layer of clothes, gather up some basic writing materials, towel off the bike, and head out. It *is* cold though, and the roads are just slippery enough to make the bike feel un-steady. I need to get in sync with my motorcycle, relax into the ride.

I focus on the thrumming of the engine and the interplay be-tween what I am doing physically and how the bike responds. In any conditions, the physics involved in riding a motorcycle is fasci-nating. At least as far as I can follow, which is only enough to appre-ciate it and ignite my imagination. I start to envision myself at one with the bike. The wind goes from icy to invigorating. I can feel the twists and turns in my gut, the tires gripping the road.

About an hour into the ride, I am in the midst of the motor-cycle high I was looking for, and as if on cue, the sun overpowers the clouds and the temperature taps up a few degrees higher than expected.

It doesn't always work like this, but it works today. The ideas I had for the article reappear in my mind and are wide awake now, ready to party. I start looking for the right place to stop, set up my computer, and take another crack at the article. I know the spot the minute I see it.

DIVIDED WE STAND

This is the part where I reflect on the year gone by. I gather up the past 12 months like two handfuls of sand, letting the good times and the bad sift through my fingers until I am left with a bit wisdom earned from another year of life and a few glimmering flakes of gold I can share with my readers. This is the part where I sprinkle those flecks into the last column of December, offering a thoughtful glance back and a confident look ahead, anticipating the new year with hope and good cheer.

Well, at least that's what I'm trying to do, but things are complicated this year. Despite the fact that I can't stand politics and it is the last subject I want to talk or write about, it is impossible for me to take an honest look back at 2016 without mentioning the presidential campaign that inundated the year, stirred all kinds of animosity, and divided us to the point that no matter who won, we were going to end up with roughly half of the population not only dissatisfied with the outcome, but devastated by it.

So ... there goes my neat little metaphor about the sands of time slipping between my fingers. A more fitting image for 2016 would be handfuls of thick, sticky mud left behind from a muckraking, mudslinging race that bothered me more than I could have imagined as I am not a political person. Sure, I stay informed and I exercise my right to vote, but that's the extent of it.

But this election hit home for me. Raised in Rimersburg and spending the majority of the following three decades as a writer living in various cities across the country, I have gathered a very mixed bag of friends, family, and acquaintances. Knowing and caring about people from a wide range of backgrounds has been a blessing, giving me different perspectives on life and introducing me to ideas and beliefs outside of anything I would have experienced on my own. These relationships added depth to my writing and to my life.

Then along comes this election not only ripping the nation in half but splitting the people I know and care about until they are standing on either side of an unbridgeable chasm and glowering at each other like enemies on the verge of war.

The ugliness started on Facebook with political posts. They were increasingly nasty and the corresponding comments often sank to the level of name-calling and stopped just short of threatening physical violence. Then, left and right, people were proclaiming, "If my posts offend you, then 'un-friend' me!" Unfortunately, a lot of un-friend-ing went on this year and not just between Facebook friends. A married couple I went to college with came close to breaking up over political differences even though they'd always been on different sides.

I hope things calm down a little now that the election is over, but as long as the division is this pronounced, there is bound to be more madness ahead. So, even though I can't dash off an end-of-the-year column that sparkles with hope and good cheer, I have come to a few conclusions that might come in handy during 2017.

As I said, I don't like talking politics, but if a person can keep a cool head and listen as much as they talk, this might be a good time for exchanging ideas. This is more about the exchange than trying to change someone's opinion. Respect is the key, and of course, being able to agree to disagree.

Looking at my divided friends, family, and acquaintances as a sort of microcosm of the country, I can say that there are some good and decent people on both sides. Not elitists and tree-huggers, not haters and hicks, but people who I know to be funny and interesting and kind. They all want the best for their country, and while their opinions of what that is vary tremendously, they are the result of their unique experiences. I don't know if we can be united anytime soon, but I do know our differences have always been our strength and any attempt to bring us back together is a worthwhile endeavor.

WHERE OPPORTUNITY LIES

According to pithy sayings and any number of maxims, opportunity knocks. And yet, this has not been my experience. Opportunity is something I hunt down like a mad dog. The search is usually long, exhausting, and often unsuccessful.

Now, I am not complaining. I have had my fair share of opportunity and believe I have made the most of it, but it certainly didn't arrive at my door with a polite tapping, which begs the question: then how did it arrive? And more importantly, how is that knowledge useful in the future?

This is of particular interest to me right now as I have been surviving on freelance jobs for the past two years. The first year was by design. I wanted to put the majority of my focus on writing my latest novel and spending time with my family. The experience was great. At the start of the second year, the plan was to go back to a full-time position, something stable, a job I could really sink my teeth into. With a mile-long resume and the willingness to relocate just about anywhere, I figured this was a relatively solid plan.

Well, you know what they say about the best laid plans of mice and men. (If you don't, it is that they "often go awry.") I am not freaking out just yet. I have been in this position many times. It is one of the downfalls of an unconventional lifestyle. The variety and adventure I seek come with considerable risk. I frequently find myself in uncharted territory and, every once in a while, I get stranded.

Looking back at the opportunities of my life, I have to say that I stumbled over the best ones. They came to me unannounced and wearing a disguise.

I have many examples of this but two of them took place simultaneously just outside of Cleveland. I was living in Los Angeles at the time. I was disillusioned and sick of the politics involved in acquiring work as an actor and getting my screenplays to the right people. At the time, the only bright spot in my career was that a community college in Ohio regularly ordered boxes of *Strip Cuts*, my first novel.

I called to thank them for their support and found out my book was a huge hit in their English classes. They asked if I would visit their school. I told them I would be happy to, and half-jokingly added, "Heck, if you got a job for me, I'll stay."

As it turned out, they were short on adjunct English teachers for the upcoming semester. Now, I was living in California, I'd never taught English before, and classes started in a few weeks. But technically, I was qualified to teach and I was ready for a change, so when they offered three classes, I went for it.

Upon arrival, a professional couple I met through the college offered to rent me a room in their house as their children had married and moved away. It was a beautiful place, but I wanted my own space, not a room in someone else's house. However, I reluctantly accepted because I was overwhelmed with so little time to prepare my classes and find an apartment.

It turned out that I absolutely loved teaching. It allowed me to rediscover my passion for reading and writing by sharing it with my students, which was just what I needed after Los Angeles. Also, I became good friends with the couple I rented off of and found out that they had a second home—even more luxurious—in Columbus. They alternated weekends between the two places and offered to let me, if I liked, spend my weekends in whichever house was vacant. And, yes, of course, I could invite a girlfriend or even throw the occasional party if I wanted.

Even though I'd only signed on for one semester, I ended up teaching there for six years.

Other opportunities were so well disguised that I initially threw them away. This was the case with the most lucrative job I've ever had. A former colleague had been hired to build a team for a two-year contract job in Washington, D.C. and offered me a spot. I was not interested in the work and didn't believe I had the necessary qualifications anyway. This guy insisted I was exactly right for it. I respectfully declined ... three times! He was persistent and made me an offer I would have been crazy to walk away from. I accepted it and he was right. It was a successful two years for all involved.

So, is there anything to be gleaned from this as I send resumes and cover letters into the abyss? Yes, I think so. Here are a few things worth remembering:

Stay alert - opportunity can come from anywhere and at any time

Be flexible – the perfect prospect might not appear that way at first so if it's close, give it a shot

Take a chance – it could be very rewarding and even if it isn't a success, you will gain experience

Keep the faith - something always comes along sooner or later, provided you don't give up along the way

WAYWARD SON: TRAVELS AND REFLECTIONS

SYNCHRONICITY

So, there I am, driving home from my girlfriend's place, feeling good, feeling alive, wishing I could have stayed longer as I sing along with a song on the radio ... which I realize is about a guy driving home from his girlfriend's place, feeling good, "feeling alive," and wishing he could have "stayed a little longer."

And that's not the weird part.

Over the past two months, there have been so many of these strange coincidences that I have come to the conclusion that there is something far more mysterious and magical than mere coincidence at play here.

No, I'm not cracking up or going all twilight zone on you, and I am not the only one who believes there is more to these so-called fluke experiences than meets the eye.

Carl Jung—the renowned Swiss psychiatrist and founder of analytical psychology—coined the term "synchronicity" to explain this phenomenon in 1930. A simplified version of this idea is that everything in the universe is connected and these "meaningful coincidences" offer a glimpse at just how connected we are and how powerful our thoughts can be in affecting the world around us.

Odds are good that you have experienced a synchronicity in your life at one point or another. For instance, if have you ever thought of someone you haven't seen in years, and then ran into them the next day, you have had a synchronicity. Another example is picking up the phone to call or text someone just as they call or text you.

This is not the first time I have experienced a series of synchronicities like this, though it is the most intense. They seem to occur during periods of strong emotion and act as a reflection—good or bad—of what is happening in my life. This brings me back to the woman's house I was driving home from at the beginning of this column.

The synchronicities started before we met when she stopped at my sister's shop to order tee-shirts for a fundraiser. "The whole time I was talking to her," my sister, Susan, said, "I just kept thinking of you."

"Why?"

"I don't know." She shrugged. "I just kept thinking that you two need to meet each other."

"Is she single?" I asked.

"I think so. And pretty."

She introduced us via text. Although I never ask a woman out without having met her in person first, I made an exception for some reason. She accepted and suggested we meet at a bar/restaurant about an hour from where I live ... that just happened to be my favorite bar/restaurant in western Pennsylvania.

We clicked instantly. Despite coming from different backgrounds and being different ages, we had some very similar experiences. We like the same eclectic mix of movies, share the same belief system, and our bucket list of cities and countries we plan to travel to are almost exactly the same. The synchronicities have been happening between us on an almost daily basis for over two months now and perhaps the most striking was remembering something I had written down last year.

Frustrated with my dating experiences at the time, I wrote down exactly the kind of woman I wanted to meet and put it in my journal. Not remembering what I'd written, I went back to it recently to find eight very specific attributes.

She has every single one of them. The list was dated almost exactly one year before we met.

Even more bizarre, when I showed her the list, she told me she'd been doing something similar, only, instead of a list, it was a painting of a couple embracing. When she showed it to me, I knew exactly how it was like my list.

Even though synchronicity cannot be scientifically proven, there are hundreds of books on the subject, speculating everything from "this is the gateway to understanding the universe" to "this is a bunch of malarkey."

Regardless of what you believe, it is a fascinating concept and fun to contemplate.

So, the next time you think of a long-lost friend and they suddenly appear or you are struggling with a problem and you randomly meet a stranger who knows the answer, you might want to take a moment to look a little closer. What are the thoughts and emotions surrounding the event or the person? Does it reflect what is going on in your life? Could these incidents be happening for a reason, telling you something, offering direction or guidance?

If you have any interesting experiences with synchronicities you'd like to share, I'd get a kick out of hearing them. Please feel free to email me at DavidDrayer.com anytime to share your story or just say hello.

ABOUT THE AUTHOR

David Drayer is the author of the novels *Strip Cuts, A Noble Story, Something Fierce,* and the novella, *Attachment.* Born in the small town of Rimersburg, Pennsylvania, he has lived in many cities and towns across the country. He holds an MFA from the University of Iowa and has worked countless jobs, including stints as a construction worker, English professor, landscaper, ghostwriter, corporate trainer, and instructional designer.

Daviddrayer.com

Made in the USA
Columbia, SC
25 June 2018